A SKEPTIC DISCOVERS

ANGELS

... ARE REAL

Bill Banks

Impact Christian Books

A Skeptic Discovers Angels . . . Are Real, Bill Banks
ISBN #0-89228-133-2
Copyright © 2003

Impact Christian Books, Inc.
332 Leffingwell Ave., Suite 101,
Kirkwood, MO 63122
314-822-3309

Cover Design: *Ideations*

March 2003 First Printing

All Scripture references are taken from the Authorized King James
version of the Holy Bible.

Printed in the United States of America

CONTENTS

Part One

THE "HITCH-HIKERS"

THE DISAPPEARING "HITCH-HIKER"...................7

David Alsobrook . . .
A MESSAGE FROM AN ANGEL NAMED "FRED".....15

Part Two

MORE AMAZING ACCOUNTS

Tom Sims 27
 I MET AN ANGEL AT THE GARDEN TOMB..........29

Roy McGown 37
 AN ANGELIC CHAUFFEUR...............................38

Scott Ward 43
 ANGELIC VAN and GASOLINE MIRACLE..............44

Joel Oliver 51
 ANGELS IN LAS VEGAS..................................52

Ted Rush 57
 TED MET MICHAEL!.......................................59

Kathy Leshe . . .   .…....71
MICHAEL APPEARS IN JERUSALEM...........…........72

Linda Clark . . .   .…....75
 AN ANGELIC GUIDE...................…........…....…......76

Michelle Pottebaum . . .   .…....81
WAS "JODY" AN ANGEL?...............…......…....82

Ruth Anderson . . .   .…....…......89
A LOOK OF DISTINCTION; EMINENCE................91

Richard Burke . . .
 THE ANGELIC BEGGAR......................…................95

Part Three

A REVELATION OF HEAVEN

Bill Banks . . .
A PERSONAL VISION OF HEAVEN: …....…..........107
          MY TWO "BROTHERS".......................108

The angel of the LORD encampeth round about them that fear him, and delivereth them.

Psalm 34:7

Bless the LORD, ye his angels, that excel in strength, that do his commandments, hearkening unto the voice of his word. Bless ye the LORD, all ye his hosts; ye ministers of his, that do his pleasure.

Psalm 103:20-21

Who maketh his angels spirits; his ministers a flaming fire.

Psalm 104:4

OTHER TITLES BY THE SAME AUTHOR

Alive Again!

Ministering to Abortion's Aftermath

Power for Deliverance: Songs of Deliverance

Deliverance from Fat

Deliverance from Childlessness

Deliverance For Children & Teens

Breaking Unhealthy Soul-Ties

Shame-Free

The Little Skunk (Sue Banks)

Everything Is Possible With God
(The Martin Hlastan Story)

How to Tap into the Wisdom of God

The Heavens Declare...

Three Kinds of Faith for Healing

Overcoming Blocks to Healing

PART ONE

THE "HITCH-HIKERS"

Back in 1994 I shared some of the observations which follow with the editor of a Christian newspaper, and as a result, he asked me to write an article for his paper. As it turned out, the article was never submitted, but it is as relevant today as it was then, and so I share it with you.

Have you heard the story of
THE DISAPPEARING "HITCH-HIKER"?

Let me preface this article by stating unequivocally that I do believe in Angels and that God still sends them today as ". . . ministering spirits, sent forth to minister for them who shall be heirs of salvation." (Heb 1:14) Although I have never personally met an angel, I do have several Christian friends who have.

Have you heard the story of the disappearing hitch-hiker? The first time I heard the story a few months ago, I rejoiced in my spirit, but at the same time, there was a vague, familiar disquietude within my spirit as well.

Let me tell you how I first heard the story. A very excited friend called me one night, who'd just heard it shared at a prayer meeting at her church. Her account went something like this...

"A lady at our church told us tonight that her hairdresser had, the day before, been driving down Highway 44 from St. Louis toward Sullivan and on the way passed a hitch-hiker alongside the road. Since she never picked up hitch-hikers, she went on past him, but then the Lord directed her to go back and pick him up. So she obediently turned her car around and went back and pulled over. The man got in the back seat of her car."

[At this point my rational mind kicked in and whispered two questions to me: "Why would a woman traveling alone pick up a hitch-hiker?" And "Why on earth would a woman traveling alone, supposedly in her right mind, allow a stranger to sit behind her in her car?" Red flag of guidance: Check number #1.]

She continued, "After some preliminary polite conversation, passing the time of day, the conversation turned to the things of God. The hitch-hiker asked if she was a Christian. And when that had been established, he told her, *". . . that Jesus is coming very soon . . . in fact, that Gabriel had placed the trumpet to his lips and was just about to blow . . ."*

"By this point the Christian hairdresser was understandably excited and turned to ask her passenger when this would occur . . . only to discover that the hitch-hiker had disappeared. She didn't know what to do then but decided to continue on her journey. Upon arriving at Sullivan, she went to the police station and reported the incident. The desk sergeant said, "You are *the eighth person* to come in here with that story this week."

[If, in fact, eight people had reported this kind of incident to the police, wouldn't some eager reporter have latched onto the story even if only to mock it? Red flag of guidance: Check #2.]

———

The account of the disappearing hitch-hiker is especially appealing to us, as Christians, because it reaffirms truths that we already believe. An additional appeal is that it tends to offer something seemingly "concrete" to add to our faith, that Jesus is indeed going to come again, and *soon*, a theme which is clearly stated frequently in the Scripture. In fact, Jesus states in Revelation four times, "*I come quickly,*" (3:11, 22:7, 22:12, and 22:70) and it is the closing theme of the Bible:

> "*He which testifieth these things saith, Surely I come quickly. Amen. Even so, come, Lord Jesus. The grace of our Lord Jesus Christ be with you all. Amen.*"

Rev. 22:20-21

———

Suddenly, I remembered why there had been that nagging familiarity and doubt that had been bothering me about this account, as much as I wanted to believe it . . . Back in the early days of the Charismatic movement in the early seventies, I had heard a number of similar 'disappearing hitch-hiker' stories. And the common denominator in the stories was that they all had the same theme or message: "JESUS IS COMING SOON!"

In the early seventies, the Body of Christ in St. Louis was abuzz with the accounts of the hitch-hiker(s). Since we, as believers, already believed that which the stories under-scored, we found them to be almost irresistible. Our hearts rejoiced with each new account.

There were many similar stories circulating around St. Louis, but mainly they were being reported as having occurred 'out east.' In fact they were so prevalent that we all wondered how long the secular press could deny such powerful, recurring, supernatural witnesses to the truths we so deeply believed.

Reader's Digest finally ran an article entitled something like "The Disappearing Hitch-hiker of Hwy. 1" by a reporter who had attempted to track down the accounts but was never able to get to the first generation of the story. It was always the "friend of a friend" who'd had the encounter. The article was not anti-Christian, but it was certainly embarrassing to many of us, who had rather gullibly accepted the accounts without verifying the sources.

=======

With these thoughts in mind, I called the Sullivan Police Department and told them I was a minister and writer from St. Louis calling attempting to verify a story I had heard of a disappearing hitch-hiker, which had supposedly been reported to them. The courteous reply of the desk sergeant was that they had no such reports at all. "However," he added with a laugh, "I wish it were true."

A few days before I called the Sullivan police station, a young woman brought her daughter to my prayer room seeking healing prayer. After ministering to them, we began sharing about the things of God and the subject of angels came up. As I began discussing the hitch-hiker story, the daughter became very excited and interrupted me saying, "I've already heard this story." Her mother encouraged me to go ahead and tell the story to see if it was the same account.

Afterward, the girl said she'd indeed heard the same story from a teacher at her Christian school. However, in her teacher's version, the woman's destination was *Warrenton*, Missouri (west of St. Louis), and the police said they'd had *ten* reports.

In the third account I heard, the difference was that the destination was *Desoto*, Missouri (south of St. Louis), and the police had received *12 reports* of disappearing hitch-hikers.

[Notice that the numerical factor in the accounts was increasing; the story kept getting "better." Red flag #3.]

Realizing that we were confronted by another Christian rumor, I was reminded of another widely circulated hoax. About thirty years ago, the rumor began to circulate that Madeline Murray O'Hare had filed a motion with the FCC to have all religious programing banned from the radio and television airwaves. Shortly, local Christians began circulating petitions opposing the O'Hare plan. All the government's protestations that there was no such bill were of no avail; the petitions kept circulating and being sent by the hundreds of thousands to Washington D.C. One of the major evening news shows carried the story of persistent rumors of the non-existent O'Hare motion and a personal appearance and appeal by the Postmaster General of the United States asking Christians to save their money and to not send any more petitions for there definitely was no such proposal before the government.

Such gullibility on the part of certain members of the Christian community reflects poorly upon all Christians, as we all tend to "be painted with the same brush."

Having been in this walk for twenty-six years, and operating a Christian bookstore during that period, I have seen the O'Hare petition movements revive about every five years, and I have had to explain the problem (hoax) to sincere, well-intentioned Christians who wanted me to display the petitions in my store.

Such gullibility and lack of discernment on the part of Christians tends to make us all look foolish and tends to weaken our credibility when we attempt to witness to the discerning unbelievers.

It is the responsibility of Christians to use their God-given brains and to pray for discernment. It is incumbent upon believers to exercise good judgment and to conduct themselves in a Godly fashion. Regrettably, many Christians are afraid to judge, due to a misinterpretation of the scriptural warning not to judge self-righteously nor hypocritically (and refers primarily to pronouncing guilt or condemning others). Believers should consider the following scriptural encouragements to exercise good judgment.

> *Judge not according to the appearance, but judge righteous judgment.*   John 7:24

> *Do ye not know that the saints shall judge the world?*

And if the world shall be judged by you, are ye unworthy to judge the smallest matters?

1 Cor. 6:2

Know ye not that we shall judge angels? How much more things that pertain to this life?   1 Cor. 6:3

But he that is spiritual judgeth all things, yet he himself is judged of no man.   1 Cor. 2:15

*   *   *   *   *

You can understand that I would naturally be suspect of any account regarding a disappearing hitch-hiker . . . However, I finally encountered an actual, verifiable, first-generation account of a disappearing hitch-hiker.

The following account comes from a well-respected Evangelist, whom I consider a friend.

> **God often does the unexpected and may employ angels to confirm His working.**

13

A MESSAGE FROM AN ANGEL
NAMED "FRED"
By David Alsobrook

This is a completely true story which happened to me, David W. Alsobrook, and which I want to share with you, my dear friends. On Sunday morning, August 25, 1996, I attended a church service at Deeper Life Assembly and was incredibly blessed by the worship and the ministry of Pastor David Gray. The anointing of the Lord was so sweet! After the meeting I got in my car and began driving to the other side of Nashville to attend another service at the Church of Antioch, which was to begin at 2:00 pm. As soon as I got on the 440 Loop heading east, I noticed a hitch-hiker on the side of the road. My custom has always been to pick up hitch-hikers and share the love of God with them, so I pulled my car over and offered the man a ride.

There's no telling how many hitch-hikers I've picked up across the years – probably hundreds. They are always tired, hungry, and fairly smelly (no criticism intended). They usually have someone they're upset with and bitter against. They invariably ask for food or money and usually welcome a nice cold drink.

Instantly, I was aware how different this man was from all the others. First he was incredibly happy and wholesome. He was clean – his clothing was neat, his face clean-shaven. He had come to Nashville all the way from Albuquerque, where he "had delivered a message from the Lord" a mere 24 hours earlier. (This would have been a near

15

impossibility.) No, he wasn't hungry and didn't want me to pull off at a nearby exit for a cold drink, either.

When he first entered my car, he took my hand and smiled warmly. His warmth literally traveled up my arm, but I thought it was the great anointing I was still under from the service I had just left. He told me his name was Fred and that he had a message for me from the Lord. "The Lord is pleased with your desire to serve Him and your desire to be filled with His love."

I began to praise the Lord, thinking that this man was a unique brother in Christ. (I honestly had no idea at that time that he was an angel.) I wondered, "How does this brother know that my heart and ministry theme for three years has been love?" I assumed he was operating in the prophetic realm. Then he called me "John" and said, "As you keep desiring to follow love, the Lord will work His love in you more and more." The power of God came on me. (There were goose-bumps on my arms.) And I thought, "How does he know I've asked the Lord to make me another John – an apostle of love?" And then, as if he knew my thought, he said, "I know your name is David, but you remind me of John."

Then Fred told me that **Jesus is coming soon and we need to always stay ready**. "Many of God's people know to avoid outward sin, but sin of the heart must be avoided, too. It's important to keep your spirit right," he told me. I agreed with him and asked him what kind of work he did. "I sow seeds and help things grow," Fred said with a smile and a twinkle in his blue, blue eyes that seemed to go on forever.

He asked if I wouldn't mind carrying him to the other side of Nashville. "It's out of my way, but I have time to do it before the next church service begins," (I thought.) So we drove on from one side of Nashville to the other, while Fred kept affirming me and quoting Scripture effortlessly. I found myself wanting to stare into his eyes – it even made me a little embarrassed. Mother always told me not to stare. Besides, I was driving! Still, I could not quit looking directly into his eyes, although it made me a little uncomfortable, because I felt that this fellow was looking right through me.

As we reached the other side of Nashville, I became a little sad. Soon this wonderful man of God would be getting out of my car. I didn't want him to leave. "Can you go to church with me this afternoon? I'll bring you right back here after the service?" "Thanks David, but I have two men to speak to tonight in Knoxville and have an appointment in Cleveland, Ohio tomorrow evening with someone else." Although I have driven all over America and should have known better, it did not seem strange to me until a few hours later, after my friend Roger Miller pointed it out to me, that the logistics of such a trip were highly unlikely – that Fred could have ministered to someone in Albuquerque Saturday, me in Nashville Sunday afternoon, two others in Knoxville Sunday evening and someone else in Cleveland on Monday and not be tired, dirty, hungry or even late! Duh! Where was my brain? All I knew was, I felt incredibly great having this complete stranger in my car. It was as though we had known each other for years. And, as I have said, I was sad that he had to go on and that we couldn't spend more time together.

I pulled over to the shoulder of I-40 East at the Briley

Parkway exit, as Fred had requested. Three days earlier I had told a local prayer partner that I had been praying to become a **kind person** at all times and in all situations. In fact, I had been praying about it all that week. A couple of hours later, during the service at the Church of Antioch, the prayer partner confirmed to everyone that I had told her this. Fred, of course, had no way of knowing this, but as he lingered with me in my car for a few minutes before exiting, he asked, "Can I take your hand and pray for you, David?" "Sure, I'd like you to pray for me." "Look at me while I pray for you." This was when *something* went right through me, right out of Fred's eyes. "Father, I thank you for David's spirit and the wonderful love you have put in his life." I just sat there in my seat, immobile. I couldn't even pray. Then as waves of wonderful warmth poured over me, Fred said, "You are a beautiful man, David, and the Lord says to tell you that He is making you a *kind person*."

I stared into those blue, blue eyes filled with heaven and said, without thinking, "I'll see you in heaven, Fred." "Yes, you will!" he beamed and opened the door. I was weeping by this time, completely overcome by the words of this stranger and the warmth of God's presence that was flooding me. As I pulled my car back out onto the highway, I looked back to see Fred, and HE WAS GONE!!!

"Do not forget to entertain strangers, for by doing so some have unwittingly entertained angels."

* * *

David reports that since he picked up "Fred" his life has dramatically changed. The Lord has confirmed everything the angel told him many times over. Since 1996, David along with his lovely wife, Ginny, has witnessed literally

18

thousands of healing miracles in his traveling ministry. The Lord has been doing amazing dental miracles of all sorts as well. David says, "I have thanked the Lord for Fred's visit hundreds of times, and still tingle whenever I remember it."

Evangelist David Alsobrook
President, Sure Word Ministries
P.O.Box 2306
Brentwood, TN 37024

David Alsobrook answered the call to minister at the tender age of 16 and entered traveling ministry the following year (1972). Since then he has seen thousands saved, healed, filled with the Holy Spirit, and delivered from bondages. He has ministered in more than 1400 different churches, camps, conferences, and special groups.

David has written 45 books which have been distributed in 50 nations. They have been translated into 28 languages. Conservative estimates of his press runs exceed four million copies. Noted leaders of the Christian community have quoted frequently from his material in their speeches and publications. His book *The Bible Truth on Abortion* has attained more than 500,000 copies in print and has been placed in numerous counseling centers. Many mothers have decided to birth rather than abort after reading this book. His other books have been read by people from all walks of life, including at least one U.S. President, and letters from people all around the world have testified of lives being enriched and changed by the power of the Word of God.

In recognition for his services to the Body of Christ, David has been awarded two honorary doctorates of divinity (1995, Christian Life School of Theology; 2001, Cathedral Bible College).

David and his wife Ginny regularly watch God perform many miracles of healing and do signs and wonders in their ministry. Since 1999 He has brought them into a new realm of His glory where He has replaced amalgam fillings with gold, platinum or new enamel. Many people receive dental miracles, including root canals and even new teeth growing in where the second tooth had fallen out. At least three persons have been removed from the Heart Transplant Waiting List, and diabetics have had their insulin prescriptions revoked. The blind have received their sight and the deaf have heard. In David's services Jesus is always exalted as the Miracle Worker in attendance.

OBSERVATIONS...

Angels are not to be sought: It is Jesus, whom we should be seeking, and desiring to see, like the Greeks.

> *And there were certain Greeks among them that came up to worship at the feast: The same came therefore to Philip, which was of Bethsaida of Galilee, and desired him, saying, Sir,* **we would see Jesus**.
>
> John 12:20 21

Although we do not seek after angels, having their reality confirmed to us does give another confirmation of God's love, concern and provision for His children, because. . .

> *Are they* [the angels] *not all ministering spirits, sent forth to minister for them who shall be heirs of salvation?*
>
> Heb. 1:14

Angels come not because we seek them, but rather they come on the basis of our need and are sent as God's messengers, emissaries or agents to accomplish His will and to further His purposes.

The title of this book is quite appropriate, for I was indeed skeptical of many modern accounts of angels, as you have learned. It is certainly true that there are many accounts that are flaky, and often some that are either marginally, or blatantly, occult.

However, I can personally vouch for the credibility of each of the individuals, whose accounts appear in this book, and who have agreed to let me share their stores with you. Most of these stories I initially heard either in my prayer room, or as they were shared publicly in our Thursday night meetings.

The majority of these people I have known for close to twenty years, some even longer. None of them are "weird" or living in a world of unreality. All of them are normal down-to-earth people, including housewives, pastors, and those simply working for a living, and I am privileged to call all of them friends.

Now prepare to have your spirits lifted even higher, and your faith built, as you read their personal accounts of angelic encounters.

PART TWO

MORE AMAZING ACCOUNTS

Almost twenty-five years ago, a young man, who at last report was serving as a YWAM (Youth With A Mission) missionary in the near east, came to our Thursday night meeting for the first time. At one point he testified, "I just saw the ceiling of this room disappear, and the entire perimeter of the ceiling was filled with angels who were seated on top of the walls and they were all listening intently. And some seemed to be taking notes."

At the time, I think I mentally dismissed his comments (perhaps, in part to refuse pride any entry) as either over eagerness on his part to be spiritual or as an attempt to ingratiate himself with the group. However, I knew that Jesus said that even *the angels of heaven did not know the hour of His coming, but only His Father knew,* and there was something about what that young man said that stayed with me. I later found a confirmation for his comment in Peter's observation:

> *Of which salvation the prophets have inquired and searched diligently, who prophesied of the grace that should come unto you: Searching what, or what manner of time the Spirit of Christ which was in them did signify, when it testified beforehand the sufferings of Christ, and the glory*

*that should follow. Unto whom it was revealed, that not unto themselves, but unto us they did minister the things, which are now reported unto you by them that have preached the gospel unto you with the Holy Ghost sent down from heaven; which things **the angels desire to look into**.*

1 Pet 1:10-12

Many years later the Lord revealed another truth to me which parenthetically added additional confirmation. In Malachi there is an amazing and virtually overlooked truth stated:

*Then they that feared the LORD spake often one to another: and the LORD hearkened, and heard it, and a **book of remembrance was written before him** for them that feared the LORD, and that thought upon his name.*   Mal 3:16

The exciting implication of this verse is that when we, believers who reverence the Lord, share with one another about the deeds, goodness, and majesty of the Lord, He causes the angels to record what is said in a "book of remembrance." That is fantastic! *Each time two or more of us gather and share about the things of God, the angels are present and are taking notes about what we have to say.* Doesn't that bless your soul?

It should be clearly understood by all Christians that angels are neither to be worshiped (Col. 2:18), nor should they be sought. Although we do not seek after angels, when their reality is confirmed to us, we have another confirmation of God's love, concern and provision for His children.

My theological resistance to the possibility of modern angelic appearances began to soften as I began encountering those who had experiences with angels.

Over the past thirty years many in my prayer room have testified of having had angelic encounters. A number of them were far too believable to dismiss. A couple of typical stories sounded like this:

> I was in the hospital as a child of four, and they were expecting me to die with a very high fever. Late one night I told my mother, who was staying overnight with me, "Look at the angel." She thought I was hallucinating due to the fever. But I felt a comfortable, refreshing warmth flowing within me, and the next morning, the doctors declared I was healed and sent me home.

> The last week of my mother's life in the hospital, she kept saying, "There are angels standing outside my door, and they are waiting for me." As she was dying, she smiled at the doorway and said, "Come on in." To the gathered family, she simply said, "They are ready for me," and she fell asleep in the Lord.

Accounts such as these are difficult to refute when related by intelligent believable people, such as Tom...

TOM SIMS

One morning I answered the phone to hear a very distressed friend on the other end of the line. "Bill, this is Judy Sims. Please pray for Tom. I just put him in a cab for the airport to go to Israel. He was so weak, I had to carry his suitcase to the cab for him. We know he had a heart attack yesterday: he got pale and passed out. But we decided that he couldn't be in any better place than with a group of pastors in the Holy Land."

We prayed in agreement for Tom. After hanging up, I reflected on Tom's testimony up to that point. In 1982 Tom, then a salesman for a well-known publishing house, had come to my prayer room and received the Baptism with the Holy Spirit. A little over two weeks later he came to one of our meetings and received a healing, which included the lengthening of a short leg and an apparent twist in his spine. Tom later had to have the suit he wore to the meeting retailored to fit his corrected body. Whenever I saw Tom wearing that suit, he would laugh and point out his "testimony suit."

Tom returned to the prayer room the next week asking, "Tell me what's wrong with Masonry?" He explained that he had been very active in the Shriners but had felt led to resign his membership two days after his healing. The same week he returned to our healing meeting to give his testimony, having resigned from all the orders of Masonry to which he belonged.

Beautifully the Lord convicted him of the errors of Masonry without human intervention. About a year and a half after receiving the Baptism of the Spirit, he was ordained as an Assemblies of God Pastor, and today heads a national ministry. But I am getting ahead of his story . . .

I MET AN ANGEL
AT THE GARDEN TOMB
By Tom Sims

Thanksgiving morning 1998, I came downstairs and got a frozen turkey out of the freezer to help my wife Judy prepare it to put in the oven. As I was unwrapping the turkey, suddenly a pain hit my chest that felt like a steamroller running over my entire body. I fell back into a kitchen chair and passed out briefly. When I awakened, I saw Judy heading for the phone to call 911. I yelled, "Stop, don't call them!"

At that point. I was sitting in a puddle of sweat – my pajamas and robe were completely soaked. She said, "I've got to call an ambulance to get you to the emergency room."

I said, "No! I'm not going to do that. Tomorrow I'm going to Israel."

The next day I was scheduled to leave with a group of pastors on a FAM trip (a familiarization trip to teach pastors the ropes about leading tours) to the Holy Land. Since I had been to Israel several times, I thought it would be helpful for me, before actually leading a tour group of our people to Israel. Needless to say, I spent most of the day in bed and my family was very upset with me, wanting me to go to the hospital.

I knew it wasn't a smart thing to do in the natural but felt strongly that I needed to make the trip to Israel, that I had to be with the other pastors, and as if God were calling me to Israel for a reason.

The next morning the cab arrived to take me to the airport. Judy helped me out to the cab and told the driver to keep an eye on me, explaining what had happened to me. The cab driver almost refused to take me under the circumstances.

However, I made it to the airport, and by the time I arrived there, I was feeling better. I met some of the other pastors, and two of my closest friends, to whom I explained what had happened, telling them not to be alarmed but to keep an eye on me. I told them I felt strongly that we needed to be together in Israel. One of the pastors was planning to videotape the entire trip and did record on video everything as we travelled.

Toward the end of our trip we wound up at the Garden Tomb where, along with another pastor, I was asked to serve Communion to the entire group. All together there were approximately twenty pastors and wives. On our trip we had each purchased an olivewood communion cup in anticipation of the planned Communion observance. Just as we were about to commence, two ladies joined our circle, and so we invited them to join us.

Some of the men said afterward that they felt there was something very unusual about the women joining us, and so did I. There seemed something surreal about what was occurring. I suggested to the pastor videotaping the service that, since we would be short two cups, that the two of us refrain and let the two guests have our cups.

However, surprisingly and mysteriously, when the cups filled with grape juice were passed around, there was a cup for each of us, even though there were two unexpected participants: God had provided two extra cups (or else He multiplied what we had)!

Before taking communion, we prayed for one another and for one another's ministries. I remember as I lifted the cup to my lips, I looked across the circle at the two women, who were standing a good twenty feet or more opposite me, and my eyes met those of one of the women. I then closed my eyes and bent forward continuing in prayer.

Although I didn't see what happened next, two other pastors did and told me afterwards what happened. Suddenly the one woman was standing next to me with her hand on my shoulder. And with my eyes still closed I heard the words, *"You are healed."* When I looked up, she was back across the circle, where she had been before. Others had seen her move across the circle and touch me. They described her movement as being smooth and instantaneous, as if she hadn't just taken slow steps across the intervening area. They described it as an instantaneous movement.

My two closest pastor friends both came up to me and said, "Tom, you were just touched by an angel." They had seen what had happened and felt it had been an angel. The others in the circle, who were praying, did not observe what took place. The only two who actually saw what happened were the pastor who was videotaping and my one other close pastor friend. I told them what I heard when she touched me, and that the words rang throughout my body, *"You are healed!"*

Incidentally, this entire occurrence was being videotaped. As soon as the words, *"You are healed,"* were spoken to me, I felt a complete rejuvenation flow throughout my entire body. I suddenly felt wonderful. As we prepared to leave, I walked over to the woman who had touched me, gave her a hug and asked where she was from. She replied in the most beautiful English, "I am from Russia. . .and I am a Russian Jew."

It blew my mind that she came and took communion with us, and yet said she was a Russian Jew. That alone was certainly unusual.

* * *

When I arrived home, right away I called my good Christian doctor, who has treated me for years. I told him I needed to see him right away, adding I had to have something checked out immediately. When I arrived, I told him exactly what had happened Thanksgiving morning when I had the heart attack. He wasn't very happy about my going on the trip without contacting him for a checkup.

He immediately took me in for tests, saying, "We have to get you right upstairs for an EKG and then get you on a treadmill for a stress test. I explained to him what had happened at the Garden Tomb and that I felt I had been healed. My good Christian doctor said, "That is hardly possible."

He did the EKG and, when he came in with the results, his face was as white as his white jacket. I didn't realize that he had been keeping a close watch on my heart, even though he had been advising me to take aspirin regularly and had seemed a bit concerned that both my mother and father had died of heart failure. He told me after the EKG that there was a spot in my heart that he had been closely watching and had been concerned about, but then he said, "Tom, there isn't anything there anymore."

I reminded him about the healing touch of God upon me and observed that God not only uses humans, but sometimes uses angels to administer His healing touch.

He still insisted that I have the stress test. When I got upstairs there were two technicians whom I had seen before – two women – one was a Muslim, one was a black Southern Baptist lady, and I told them my story. They said "Let's check this out." After the stress test, they said, "You have never gone this long, this hard and this fast before. Your heart is perfect." This was another confirmation for the doctor.

* * *

Two weeks later all those who had been on the Israel trip gathered with their wives for a little reunion at the church of one of the pastors. After dinner, they showed the videotape from the trip. I was waiting expectantly for the portion with the communion service at the Garden Tomb. I was anxious to be able to again see, and relive my healing touch and to visually share the experience with my wife and the group, and to tell them the details of the medical confirmations of my healing.

However, when the camera panned and showed the complete group gathered for communion, you could see me clearly when I bent forward, just as the woman touched me and I heard the words, *"You are healed!"* But the two women are nowhere to be seen in the videotape. Twenty of us saw them, when we invited them to join us. Two witnessed the one woman touch me....but their images do not appear on the tape.

I feel God has a real sense of humor. I had always believed that God only created *male* angels, and isn't it interesting that he sent a *woman* angel to apply His healing touch upon me.

Angels take many guises, yet always do good, always reflect the compassionate nature of the God whom both they and we serve. By their very presence they often teach us and sometimes change our attitudes.

Rev. Tom Sims

In the metropolitan St. Louis, Missouri area, Tom and Judy Sims operate Metro-Vision Ministries which presents the Gospel of Jesus Christ to children and their families. They conservatively estimate that their program of taking the gospel to the streets and into neighborhoods via their specially equipped "Jesus and Me" ministry trailers has resulted in thouands of children inviting Jesus Christ into their hearts.

Each year they also furnish several fully equipped Ministry Stage Trailers to deserving, qualified and trained Mission Outreach Ministries across the nation. In addition to donations, their ministry is funded by two Stuff-N-More resale Outreach Centers which they operate in House Springs and High Ridge, Missouri.

In addition to operating an urban Bible Training Center, they also offer ministry to Nursing Homes, the Homeless, Senior Citizens, Prisons, Families and Children.

Metro-Vision Ministries Inc.
Headquarters:1692 Carman Road, Manchester, MO 63021
Office phone 636- 230-3544

ROY MCGOWN

Roy is one of the sweetest, most humble, soft-spoken, unassuming brethren it has been my pleasure to know. We first met when he showed up at one of our Thursday night healing meetings after some of the members of his church had attended and been healed.

I have known Roy for well over twenty years and have spoken in his church. When I began considering writing this book, I remembered the story which he had shared with me about the bus and asked if he'd be willing to share it again . . .

> Angels often don't appear with wings, but appear to us as normal human beings, as our fellows, to identify with us and to aid us. Angels help, comfort, remove fear and minister to the needs of the saints, especially in assisting men to accomplish tasks for God.

AN ANGELIC CHAUFFEUR
By Roy McGown

This encounter happened back about 1989. I went on a YMCA Club 44[1] trip to see the historic sights surrounding our country's founding. There was a group of about seventy people primarily from our local areas of Kirkwood and Webster Groves, Missouri on the tour.

We were all looking forward to seeing the sights, as our bus took us through Pennsylvania. We managed to get to Philadelphia, where we saw Independence Hall and the Liberty Bell. Our plan was then to proceed west from Philadelphia a little over 130 miles to Gettysburg, but our bus began giving the driver trouble. It would frequently chug and stall.

Because of the problems with the bus, we made a decision to cut short the day's travel plans — to not try to make it to Gettysburg, and to instead go directly to Washington, D.C. where we were scheduled to spend the night.

We continued having a lot of trouble with the bus. It kept breaking down, and the driver was struggling to keep it running. The bus was having such trouble that we felt pretty sure it wasn't going to make it. So I got together with

[1] Editors note: I had heard of the YMCA's Club 44 in Kirkwood for several decades and always thought it had been named for Interstate Highway I-44, which passes through Kirkwood. However, in talking with Roy, I learned that Club 44 was originally formed as a club for youth and received its name because the club bus could only seat 44 passengers, and thus, the group was limited to 44 members.

Mike Whitson and his wife Princess, Kenneth Hinkle and others, who were in agreement with us, and we prayed and asked the Lord to work things out for us.

This all happened toward the end of July and it was very, very hot and humid. The windows on the bus would not open, so we couldn't get any ventilation and decided to have everyone get off the bus while the driver worked on the engine. We were concerned about some of the older passengers and wondered if they would be able to stand the heat.

Shortly after we prayed, we began unloading. As soon as we got the last person off the bus, another bus pulled up behind our disabled bus, and I noticed the driver was wearing a chauffeur's cap. He opened the door and said, *"I'll be your driver now. Get in, and I'll take you wherever you want to go."*

Initially, we assumed that since our driver had been having so much trouble with the bus that either the driver or someone on the bus had called the bus company on a cell phone to report the problems and had asked them to send another bus to pick us up.

We were all delighted to see him and to get on his well running air-conditioned bus. We told him that we wanted to go to Washington, D.C. He then drove us right to our hotel.

After we got to our rooms, we began discussing the events and how quickly our prayer had been answered. I suggested to Joe Cole that we ought to call the bus company to thank them and to compliment them on their service in rescuing us by sending the second bus and to compliment the bus driver on his politeness and courtesy. Although I had not noticed the name of the second bus company, Joe had gotten both the driver's number and the name of the bus company and had written them down.

We tried to find the company in the phone book, but there was no listing. We called information and learned that there was no such company. We then checked and learned that no one from our bus had called the bus company to report our difficulties. So we concluded that the Lord had sent an angel to *chauffeur* us to our destination.

* * *

I had another encounter with what I took to be an angel about four years ago. I was driving out Highway 66, now I-44, to the jail at Pacific where I went every week to hold a Bible study with the men imprisoned there. On this particular evening, I was driving my old blue 1994 Chevy pickup truck and a tire blew, just before I got to the Six Flags exit. Since the evening traffic was heavy and there was no good place on the highway to change a tire, I took a chance and drove on the flat, until I could get off the highway and to a station where I could safely change the tire.

When I looked at the tire, both it and the wheel were pretty mangled. I thought, "I'm going to have a hard time making it to the jail in time for my meeting there."

I found that the heat created by driving on the rim had apparently swollen the lugs, and I could not get a single one of them loose. I put an old blanket down on the ground, so as to keep my suit pants clean, while I knelt to get better leverage as I struggled with the lug wrench. When I knelt, I prayed, " Lord, you know that I can't get these lug nuts off the truck, I need your help." I then stood up and looked around.

Suddenly a young man with long flowing hair appeared as he stepped around the front of my truck and asked, "Do you need any help?"

Grateful for the possibility of assistance, I replied, "I sure do. My lug nuts are stuck, and I can't get them loose."

The young man said with a laugh, "I'll help you get them off, and I'll change your tire." With that he knelt down and easily removed the lugs nuts with no apparent effort. He then put the spare on the wheel and put the damaged tire in the back of the truck. When he had completed the task, he turned to me and said, matter-of-factly, *"Now, I think you'll be able to make it in time for your meeting."*

I cleaned my hands and then turned to thank the young man, and he was nowhere to be seen. I even went inside the station looking for him and into the adjoining restaurant to see if he had somehow slipped in there without my noticing. But he was nowhere to be found.

Amazingly, when I arrived at the prison, I was right on time. I concluded that this disappearing Good Samaritan was also an angel.

Pastor Roy McGown

Today Roy McGown and his wife co-pastor **New Covenant Full Gospel Church** at 7425 Virginia in St Louis, Missouri.

His church was formerly located in Kirkwood, Missouri for twenty-four years. Now they offer weekly services with Sunday School at 10:30 and Worship at 11:30 on Sundays. In addition there are Wednesday night prayer and Bible study at 7:00 p.m. and Friday night services devoted to Christian living and Christian growth.

They also actively attempt to minister to the victims of alcohol and drug addition problems and seek to reach youth with a variety of outreach endeavors.

SCOTT WARD

I'd heard of Scott's faith ministry for several years from my son Steve, who met him while working in Budapest when Scott approached him on the street to witness to him. Steve said they hit it off right away, sharing a common faith.

I first met him when he flew to the States to be in Steve's wedding in April of 2000. As we met, he was rejoicing that the Lord had again provided free transportation for him – this time he flew to the States in a cargo plane along with ninety thousand pounds of roses!

Knowing of his faith ministry and the almost daily miracles which God has worked in sovereignly opening doors for him, as well as providing free accommodations and often free transportation both for him and his team, I asked Scott if he had ever encountered any angels. He replied that he had on numerous occasions and related several experiences. Three of my favorites of his accounts are . . .

> We all recognize the validity of the old adage, "Where God guides, God provides." However, Scott's experiences with angels illustrate a second great aspect of that truth: "The greater the need, the greater the provision."

ANGELIC VAN AND GASOLINE MIRACLE

We were in Ireland and we had just had our third little boy. The Lord had supplied a vehicle to drive to Hungary, which would be our next mission field. In order to get there we took a ferry from the south of Ireland to Cherbourg. When we got off the ferry, it was about 6 o'clock in the evening. I had no French francs, and in France nothing was open to help me change any of my money into French francs. I didn't know what to do because my gas tank was on empty. The needle on the gauge was already on the line that said "empty," and the light was just about to turn on. And at the gas stations that I went to, the employees said they would not help, as I had no French money.

So I prayed desperately and claimed the story of Elijah and the women of Zarapath with the cruse of oil and barrel of flour that never ran out (1Kings 17). So then I started driving, and every once in a while I'd get off the highway to try to find a gas station that would help me change my money (as I didn't have a visa card or anything like that). But everywhere I went they said, "No!" So I had to get back on the highway and keep driving.

Within about 15 minutes of driving the warning light came on, and then I just kept driving. I drove for thirty more minutes… then 45 minutes… then an hour… then an hour and a half… then two hours! By that time I started shaking, because I was so excited at all the Lord was doing, and I knew what a miracle it was. It was about eight o'clock at night by that time.

I got off the highway to try one more gas station as there were very few towns along that road. I got back on because the people at the gas station said "No" again. I noticed that every time I got back onto the highway, there was a van that was either behind us or in front of us. I didn't really understand it, especially since it had Irish license plates, as if it had followed us from Ireland on the ferry, which kept me wondering. I just kept driving.

Another hour went by. It was nine o'clock. Then 9:30, then 10:00 p.m. I had driven four hours on empty, and I was just "flipped" out. I was hyperventilating. I was shaking; it was such a neat miracle. It was so incredible what the Lord was doing. Then I noticed the van still behind me. Then I got off the highway one last time and when I got back on, and he was right in front of me. The van should have long since passed me, but instead it was right here.

Then all of a sudden I started getting a check that maybe this vehicle had some angelic connection to the reason we weren't running out of fuel. So I started driving the car a little bit faster to just look in the window of the van. I sped up and looked in the driver's side, and no one was driving! I slowed down, totally freaked out, and went around the van on the other side, and then I saw an angel wing hanging out of the window.

Then I pulled back and slowed down for a second and let him go a moment ahead. Just at that moment the van started speeding up. By this point it was eleven o'clock at night, but on this highway the light was good, and because of the lighting on the highway, it made it possible to see miles ahead. The van just went over a little hump right in front of us, about a space of a block away. For a moment we couldn't see the van. Then as soon as we came to the hump and got over it, the van was gone. And then, boom we ran out of gas!

The car drifted over to the side. On this highway there were no houses, nothing. But just where the car had drifted and come to a stop there was a gate. We went through the gate and down a short path to a house where everyone was still wide awake, even the children, at eleven o'clock at night. They were having a birthday party with two families and some children. They spoke English and they said, "Oh sure, come. We'll fill you up." And they took us to a gas station and filled our tank and we were on our way.

And that is the story of the miracle van and the angel that kept filling up our tank.

ANGEL WITH SHEPHERD'S CROOK

When I was a missionary in New Delhi, India, one day I was out witnessing and hitched a lift with a young man from Kashmir. I witnessed to him during the entire journey. Finally he had to drop me off, because he was going to turn a different direction. When I faced him to ask if he'd like to pray to receive Jesus, he agreed and pulled over to the side of the road. Suddenly, from my left side there appeared at my window about ten little children, totally possessed. They were screaming at the top of their lungs, banging on the window with their hands, scratching at the window with their fingers and screaming incessantly at the top of their lungs. I could see this was begining to make the young man impatient and knew that we might not have enough time to pray.

I put my hand against the window and just prayed a silent prayer: "Jesus, please send those kids away right now, so this man will be able to pray with me, in Jesus' Name." About 20 seconds later, from out of nowhere appeared a seven-foot tall man, dressed like Moses or one of the prophets, with a huge shepherd's rod. He was dressed in a cloak and looked as if had come right out of Bible times. He had a big, long white beard as well, just as you'd imagine on one of the prophets.

He put the rod in between the children and the car and backed them away. It seemed as if he had a special power over them, so that they were unable to go around the rod. They were still making noise, but they had to back up as he kept pushing them backwards, away from the car.

I turned and prayed with the young man. He accepted Jesus and I took his address for follow-up.

We were then in a part of southern New Delhi that at the time was almost desolate. You could see three miles in every direction; there was nothing—no buildings, nothing for miles. I got out of the car and looked around. About a block away I could see those children. There were no other cars around, and there were no other people. And the man Who had helped us by keeping the kids away, the man that looked like one of the prophets of old, was nowhere to be seen.

ANOTHER TESTIMONY

I was out one day, street witnessing in the business section of New Delhi, telling people about Jesus, and giving out tracts. I had a whole stack of tracts that I planned to give out. Suddenly, a Hindu man approached me, and as I handed him a tract, he grabbed all the tracts from my hand, tore them up and threw them on the ground.

Then from out of nowhere, on my left side, I suddenly saw a seven-foot tall character, who just looked at the Hindu man in front of me and without saying a word. But it was as if the Hindu man understood exactly what he was thinking or saying in his mind. He humbly looked at the tracts on the ground and immediately changed. He picked up the tracts and put them back in my hand and apologized. Then I looked to my left and the seven-foot tall man had disappeared.

Scott Ward

Scott Ward leads an Africa-wide missionary organization known as Africa-Missions. Beginning in Nigeria, Scott and his team have been planting missionary bases in numerous African countries and now operate from a base in South Africa. Their heart and mission is for the most devastated countries, and they are in the process of taking the news of Jesus Christ to the war-torn countries of Africa, including Sierra Leone, Liberia, Angola, the Democratic Republic of Congo (DRC), Somalia and the Sudan.

Scott and his colleagues literally go where no one else wants to go, often in the midst of humanitarian catastrophes and armed conflict. In 2002 they brought the news of the gospel to Goma, DRC following Africa's deadliest volcano eruption in 25 years. In addition, they have been active in Sierra Leone and Liberia and have been able to minister to refuges and forced amputees from the civil war, as well as to the displaced child-soldiers. They have also made pioneering trips into the Sudan to bring the good news of Hope to the hurting population.

Information on Scott's ministry and details for making donations can be found on the website, **www.Africa-missions.org**. His ministry office telephone number is (South Africa) 011-27-72-228-3283, and his email address is **info@africa-missions.org.**

JOEL OLIVER

I have had the pleasure of ministering in Joel's church, Trinity Christian, on several occasions and have seen the Lord move mightily providing both miracles and healings during those services. I have known Joel and Sherry and their children for more than twenty years.

I remember Joel sharing the following account in our weekly healing meeting shortly after it occurred . . .

> God often uses angels to bring His peace to bear upon a situation, and also thereby ministers healing.

ANGELS IN LAS VEGAS
By Joel Oliver

In 1984 I was the Director of Pharmacy Services at Oral Roberts City of Faith Hospital in Tulsa, Oklahoma. I was also the founder and President of Joel 2:28 Ministries and one of the founders of the then fledgling Christian Pharmacist Fellowship International. I was invited to present a Pharmacy Paper at the American Society of Hospital Pharmacy Mid-Year Clinical Conference in Las Vegas in December of 1984. It was also an opportunity to help host a prayer breakfast for the Christian Pharmacist Fellowship International at the same meeting. This was a wonderful opportunity to mix my faith and my profession together at a meeting that was always fun to attend, was professionally profitable and spiritually rewarding.

My lecture was at the MGM Grand Hotel, so I booked my room in that hotel. The moment I walked through the doors of the MGM Grand Hotel, I could sense a heavy spirit. The front lobby opens into an enormous gambling casino with people drinking and gambling in every direction. I had a knowing in my heart that this meeting would be more difficult than I thought, that I was in enemy territory, and that I was not welcome there. I would be in for a spiritual battle that would challenge my faith.

I arrived at the hotel on a Tuesday afternoon. The CPFI Prayer Breakfast was scheduled for 8:00 A.M. on Wednesday morning, and my lecture was scheduled for 9:30 A.M. on that same day. I checked into the hotel and went directly to my room. I checked on the arrangements for the prayer breakfast and had an early dinner with some friends. My intention was to get back to my room early, prepare myself for the prayer breakfast, study the notes for my lecture and get to bed early. At around 10:00 P.M., I began to feel sick to my stomach. By 10:30 P.M. I began to have piercing pain in my lower back above my left kidney. The pain grew into such intense pain that I thought I was on the verge of passing out. By 11:00 P.M. the pain was almost unbearable. I had the thought that I could die in that hotel room and no one would know about it, until my body was found.

I had started to pray at 10:00 P.M. When I first began to feel sick, it became clear to me that this was both a spiritual attack and a physical attack on my life. I intensified my prayer focus and cried out for direction and deliverance. When I next looked at the clock, it was 1:00 A.M. and I was desperate for God's touch. I knew it was too late to call home, since it was 2:00 A.M. Tulsa time, and I didn't want to wake my wife Sherry. The only person that I knew who would still be up at that hour was my night pharmacist at the City of Faith Hospital Pharmacy. John Taylor is a precious Spirit-filled Baptist pharmacist, and he was scheduled to work that night. I knew John and I could get into agreement in prayer, so I called him. We prayed and John gave me this word: "You are in a spiritual battle for your life. Don't stop praying and praising God, and you will see a great victory."

I took that word seriously and continued in fervent prayer from 1:00 A.M. to 4:00 A.M. As the pain increased, I increased the fervency of my praying and the passion of my worship. At 4:00 A.M. I was at the end of myself and knew I was about to pass out from the pain. I opened my eyes and through my tears saw a brilliant light all throughout my room. When my eyes were fully open, I was amazed at what I saw.

I looked around the room and saw seven angels standing with their arms on their hips. Their elbows were touching each other so that there was no break between them as their bodies circled the whole room. The seven angels were as tall as the ceiling of the room and had powerfully built bodies. I could only make out the facial features of what appeared to be the largest angel. They each had an intense glow around their heads, waists and feet. I waited for one of the angels to speak, but none of them uttered a word. The largest angel finally looked directly at me and smiled and shook his head in an up and down motion, as if to signal "Yes." I immediately had a knowing that I was in a spiritual battle for my life, that they had been sent to guard me and to fight for me, and that I was now safe.

I don't know if I passed out at 4:00 A.M., or if I simply fell off into sleep because I was exhausted. The next thing I remembered was the phone ringing at 6:30 A.M. with my wakeup call. When I opened my eyes, the angels were gone, and the room had a pleasant smell to it. I expected to feel horrible, considering the pain I had experienced and that I had only gotten two and a half hours of sleep. When I checked myself out, I was amazed. I had absolutely no pain, and I felt as though I had just awakened from the best night's sleep I had ever had. I bounded out of bed, was filled with energy and had an overflowing joy.

Needless to say, the prayer breakfast was fantastic. The Christian Pharmacist Fellowship International is now a mature and vital organization. My lecture was also one of the best I have ever presented.

Perhaps the greatest blessing of all was the demonstration of God's love to me and the confirmation of His word in Psalm 91.

> *For he shall give his angels charge over thee, to keep thee in all thy ways. They shall bear thee up in their hands, lest thou dash thy foot against a stone.*
>
> Psa. 91:11-12

Joel A. Oliver has an earned Doctorate in Clinical Pharmacy from the University of Tennessee. From 1972 to 1985 he was the Director of Pharmacy at DePaul Hospital, Jewish Hospital, and St. John's Hospital all in St. Louis, Mo. He was the director of Pharmacy at the City of Faith Hospital in Tulsa, Oklahoma. He was an Adjunct Professor at the University of Iowa and at the St. Louis College of Pharmacy.

He was the founder and President of Joel 2:28 Ministries and was one of the founders of the Christian Pharmacist Fellowship International

He is the founder, President and Senior Pastor of **Trinity Christian Assembly of God Church** in St. Louis, Mo. (1985 to present) He is an ordained minster with the Assemblies of God. He is currently the President of Virtue House Ministries, President of Trinity Lay Bible School, Executive Board Member of Mission Metro St. Louis, and is a Master of Arts Degree Candidate at Trinity Theological Seminary. He and his wife Sherry do "Marriages That Succeed Seminars" nationally and internationally. He has been married to Sherry E. Oliver for 33 years and has four children.

Trinity Christian Assembly of God Church is located at 4720 Jamieson, St. Louis, Mo 63109. You may reach him at 314-752-1015.

TED RUSH

"Bill, have you met Ted Rush, yet?" several women asked of me as I arrived about thirty minutes before I was to speak at a healing and deliverance conference being held at Steve Bell's church in Euless, Texas.

"Who is Ted?" I inquired, assuming him to be a member of the local fellowship. (I later learned he was a pastor from Beaumont expected to attend.)

"Ted is the man who met *Michael*," they explained, as if I should have known.

"Michael? Michael who? Michael Jackson?" I asked, displaying just how "spiritual" (or prone to skepticism) I am.

"Michael, the angel," they explained, as if I were dim-witted.

"You mean he met Michael, *the Archangel?*" I asked, incredulously.

"Yes!" was the unanimous reply. Later as I was sitting in one of the pews waiting to be introduced, someone tapped me on the shoulder and said, "Meet Ted Rush."

I turned around to see a sweet-faced brother seated behind me wearing a big grin. We shook hands and then he pulled up his right pants leg, and, pointing to a grayish area about two inches or more in diameter, said, "Feel that."

A bit reluctantly I succumbed and touched the gray area, which had a grainy feel to it. "That's where Michael healed me," Ted proclaimed firmly.

I was then introduced, which interrupted our conversation, but I could hardly wait to hear the rest of Ted's story. . .

Angels are sometimes sent as God's agents both to bless and to administer healing.

TED MET MICHAEL!
By Ted Rush

I went around from church to church introducing churches and pastors to Salt International, our ministry to single people. When doing so, I often took other individuals or ministers along with me to share their testimonies of the value that the ministry had been to their own ministries.

I had been out ministering in a church with a sister in the Lord, Sandra Duncan, and afterwards returned to her house for lunch. While I was having lunch, I had an open-eyed vision, which was just as clear as if I was watching television. I had been a combat medic in the service and went out on many calls to pick up bodies. In one instance we had to pick up the body of a plane crash victim. Every bone in the individual's body was broken, and when we lifted him his whole body shook like Jell-O.

While eating with Sandra, I had a vision of a great big hand holding a large cottontail rabbit with every single bone in his body broken, just lying across his Lord's hand. I also saw two other rabbits in the vision, as if they were facing one another, but one became superimposed upon the other, and they were sitting in tall meadow grass. Then I noticed in front of the high meadow grass, a fox stalking the rabbits. For some reason, instead of asking for the Lord's interpretation, I assumed the three rabbits represented my three sons.

Concerned by the vision, I called and managed to reach

two of my sons, and they told me that their brother had just left with some friends in a Jeep to go 'mudding.' Probably within 15 - 20 minutes, the driver flipped the Jeep, killing the driver and badly injuring two others. My son, who was not injured, called 911. I didn't learn what had happened until two days later. However, having seen the vision, I had prayed for my sons until I received peace about them in my spirit.

My initial interpretation of the dream may have saved my son's life, by causing me to pray for him. But I was to learn that the correct interpretation did not involve my sons, but rather myself: I was the broken rabbit.

This occurred on a Sunday, and the next morning, Monday, a friend of mine, a Baptist preacher Scott Chandler, called and said, "Let's go horseback riding."

I asked him, "Do you have a horse big enough to carry me, because I am a large man and don't want to come back carrying the horse?"

I attempted to make a further excuse, explaining to Scott, "I can't go, because I have six counseling appointments today." When I said I couldn't go, he suggested that I reschedule the counseling and all of the people happily agreed.

I failed to yield to the little voice that said, "You haven't asked Me if you can go." To which I replied, "Yes, Lord, but I will ask," and then went on my way.

I met Scott and his fiancé Judy. (They turned out to be the other two rabbits; I was the broken rabbit.) I met them about 12 miles from my home. When we got in Scott's truck, I said, "We haven't prayed about this trip yet."

"Yes, we need to pray," they agreed. But then we got involved in conversation and forgot to pray.

By way of background, I used to rodeo and sky-dive. I raced motorcycles until I was forty-six years old. In the past I have been healed of a broken back and always carry a fold up cane with me on my motorcycle or in my car. God warned me once again in that still small voice, *"You should take your fold up cane."* But I didn't heed the warning, saying to myself, "I don't need it."

We saddled three horses. Then Scott put his finger on my horse's nose and said, "I take authority over you, you devil. You're not going to act up."

Immediately, however, when I got in the saddle, my horse began to rear up. He just kept going up, until I realized with shock that the horse was going to fall over backwards. Sensing that, I threw myself off the horse, and did a "parachute roll" as I'd been taught in the service, attempting to escape the horse's fall.

As I fell, I claimed the promise of *the body of Christ — that not a bone of his body shall be broken.* The horse fell back on its haunches and back end, but instead of rolling in the direction it was falling, it rolled in my direction, and rolled across my right leg about three inches above the ankle. I was wearing a pair of Spanish riding boots which come up almost to the knee. You could hear the snapping of the bone for a hundred yards.

Scott dismounted and starting running toward me, and as I stood up, I fainted. When I came to, Scott and Judy had removed my boot. Because they had, I could clearly see the misalignment of the bone in my leg. They both said, "It is broken."

I replied, "It is not. I am the body of Christ – it is not broken. I am not going to move by sight but by the Word of God."

What I'm saying might not be valid for anyone else, but for me, it was what I was called to do. Scott wanted to get his truck and take me right to the hospital, but once again I said, "No, it is not broken – God is my healer."

Then, I guess my rodeoing background and pride kicked in, and I said, "No horse is going to throw me." And I mounted the horse (The pain was excruciating at first.) and rode it for the rest of the day.

During the afternoon several times I had to dismount to relieve myself and each time you could hear the pieces of bone crackling and grating against each other. I thought Scott was going to go through the roof. He said repeatedly, "Ted, let me take you to the hospital."

Each time I simply replied, "No, I am healed by the stripes of Jesus."

I had a meeting later that afternoon about 40 miles from where we were riding. When I got back to Scott's house, we removed my boot and put the broken leg in a bucket of ice. By this time, it was black, purple, green and yellow. You could still clearly see the misalignment of the bone.

When I fell, my shirt had gotten muddy and grass stained, so I called my friend Sandra Duncan, because she had been doing some sewing for me, and asked if she had replaced the buttons on a shirt that I needed. She said she had and brought the shirt to Scott's place. With her help and Scott's, we were able to get the boot back on, even though the foot and leg had begun to swell badly.

By the time we got to the meeting, about sixty members of Salt International were gathered there, and the rumor had already spread that I'd had a horse fall on me. People were asking me about it, and I kept telling them that the leg was not broken.

The Lord says that He *creates the fruit of our lips* (Isa. 57:19). We are snared by every idle word that we speak. The Word also says if any tongue rises against us in judgement, we are to condemn it. So I denied to others what they were saying and politely rebuked them saying, "*I am the body of Christ and not a bone of His shall be broken,* and *by His stripes I was healed.*"

The fall happened on a Monday, and that Friday I spoke before two separate chapters of our organization and stood and jumped on that leg, which held me up. From the day of the accident, I never spoke about it, and I wouldn't let anyone else speak of it, as broken. When I jumped on the leg, that stopped the rumors.

Sandra Duncan and I were sister and brother in the Lord, and she is the only person who saw my leg other than myself. With tears in her eyes, she doctored my leg with Aloe Vera for nearly three months. But it wasn't getting better: it was getting worse. I was in dentistry at that time, operating a dental lab. A dear dental friend and business associate asked, "Ted, what's wrong with your leg?"

I asked, "What leg?"

He responded, "The one that nearly buckled on you, when you got out of the car." Recognizing the signs of gangrene on my leg, he continued, "Ted, you're not a fool, you know what that is."

Yes I knew, but I also know what the Word of God says . . . and, it was settled deep inside of me – It was not just words, not merely a foolish gesture. I knew deep down inside me that I was healed. You could not shake my faith. It was established, like concrete. Yes, I had a leg that looked bad, but the Word of God is stronger than any two-edged sword. I continued to speak life, and not death, over my situation. Stating that my leg was healed in the name of Jesus!

It appeared to be worse. It was not getting better – gangrene had set in. Having been a combat medic in the service, I knew gangrene. Gangrene is dead flesh. Eventually the dead flesh begins to make blisters. As long as the blisters are intact, you are okay, but when they begin to break open – it is just rotting flesh. Once they break, there are only two choices: amputation or death. I told Sandra that I had no insurance; the only insurance I carried was liability on my car because it was required by law in my state.

After three months of Sandra caring for my leg, we had become close friends and had even had a few dates. She kept supporting me through her tears.

One day I woke up and saw water blisters. I called Sandra, and told her I'm coming by to get a hug, and then I'm heading for Houston, because I need to go to the bank, as I only have eight quarters on me. She knew without me telling her that I was going to the Veterans Hospital.

I got on my kickstart motorcycle. As I kicked it on, I spoke to the Lord and said, "You promised that I would not be tempted beyond the measure that I could stand, but I cannot stand this any longer." I set off for Sandra's house. Normally I would have gone the city route through town but knew I would hit more traffic at that time of day, and a little voice told me to take another route.

As I sped down the highway on my motorcycle, I noticed a very small man approaching me, who appeared to be about 30 years old, wearing jeans and a brown tweed wool jacket. He was probably not more than five feet tall and probably not much more than 100 pounds. He was walking toward Beaumont, where I was coming from, but he was hitchhiking toward Port Arthur which was the direction I was headed.

Whenever I see someone walking along the highway, I automatically look to see if I can spot the person's broken down vehicle. I saw none and so I went on past the man. But, as soon as I passed him, I heard an inner voice saying, *"Go back and pick him up."*

So I made a U-turn, rode back up to him and asked where he was headed. He said, "I am going to Corpus Christi."

I said, "Man, you can't get to Corpus Christi from Port Arthur. That coastal highway has been washed out by a storm."

He said, "That's okay, I'll go to Port Arthur with you."

He got on and I began doing those zigzag curves, I often see motorcyclists doing, which is attempting to check the balance and response of the machine to the weight so that if an emergency should arise, the driver will know how the bike will act. But my motorcycle felt exactly the same with him on with me, as if he wasn't there. I was somewhat frightened because my bike wasn't responding to the added weight. I dropped my right hand down to my side, but I didn't feel anything, which was strange because normally I would have felt the passenger's knee. So, I turned my head, looked back and saw that he was still there.

Approaching Port Arthur, I crossed over a freeway interchange at Highway73 which goes to Winnie, and from Winnie you can go to Galveston and from Galveston you can reach Corpus Christi. I stopped and pointed the route out to the young man and gave him directions on how to get to Corpus Christi. He asked for a dime for a cup of coffee. (I've never had a drink of coffee and therefore had no idea of the cost, but a dime didn't sound like enough.)

I reached in my pocket and pulled out all but two of my eight quarters, and handed them to him, saying, "I don't have much. I'm Ted and I bless you in the name of Jesus."

What I said struck me as strange, because I would normally introduce myself, "I'm Ted Rush," giving my full name.

The stranger said, "I'm Michael . . . and *I bless you* in the name of Jesus."

When he turned away, I let my clutch out and went about five feet. Then suddenly, I had a 'knowing' to turn around.

And when I did and looked back, Michael was gone! He was simply no longer there. I could see for two to three hundred yards in every direction without so much as a bush to block my view.

Instantly, I also knew that I was healed. I just sat there for a while and wept.

I knew it was too late to catch Miss Duncan at her home ,so I went to her place of business. When I arrived, one of the other women, who worked there, met me and said, "Ted, Sandra has been having me pray for you, but she didn't say what to pray for." She then asked, "What have I been praying for?"

I pulled off my boot to show her, and for the first time in three months, my leg was straight as an arrow. The gangrene which had been a concern was still there, but the bone was straight. So I didn't give the gangrene any further thought.

Within three days the gangrene blisters healed up without ever peeling. I still have the discolored mark on my leg as a reminder of the time that God sent an angel to heal me.

I walked out this healing for three months - and I like to warn people to be on guard to protect the word of healing that is within you – because the enemy will try to convince you that it didn't happen or isn't real, but my healing happened! And, I have witnesses to the facts: Sandra Duncan, Scott Chandler Baptist minister, his fiancé Judy Tharp, and Dr. Jesse English, DDS were all witnesses to my broken leg and to the fact of its being healed.

* * *

For almost a year I thought that the angel that I encountered had another mission awaiting him in Corpus Christi, but I was wrong.

You will recall that as I fell from the horse, I said, "I claim *the body of Christ*: not a bone of his body shall be broken."

Years later it was brought to my attention that *Corpus Christi* in Spanish means **the body of Christ**. The angel told me, "I am going to the body of Christ." – That is who you are, and who I am – ***the Body of Christ***.

Ted Rush

In December of 1976 Ted Rush had a Damascus Road type encounter with Jesus Christ that lasted from sun up until sundown. The Lord told him to prepare himself, because he would not always be a Dental technician.

The Lord also told him he would be a teacher. Ted responded, "That would be difficult." Because at the time he could neither read nor write. Within days, he was offered a teaching position at a local university to teach Dental Materials and Laboratory Procedures. Ted then went to Pastor Larry Meaux and a dentist friend, Willie Andrepont,DDS, who has an awesome gift of healing, and asked them to pray that he could learn to read – within five weeks he had read the Bible from Genesis to Revelation. He began preparing himself for the ministry that the Lord had in store for him.

On July 8, 1981 the Lord told him to go to Belfast, Ireland. The following morning, Ted closed his successful business of 16 years within fifteen minutes. Since that time he has lived entirely by faith.

Along with his wife Nelda, in addition to operating a food ministry for the needy, he conducts seminars with a team of ministers teaching parents how to protect their children from child molesters, and he has also traveled to seventeen countries and to most of the States teaching the Gospel and making it come alive with drama.

Today he operates, and can be reached at
Fisherman's Christian Crusades
2442 McFaddin
Beaumont, TX 77702
409-832-7495

KATHY LESHE

I have known Kathy and most of her family since the early Seventies.

One of my favorite stories involving Kathy occurred while on a trip to Spain, when she and two women friends took a ferry over to Tangiers in Morrocco. One of the other ladies did not believe in the gift of tongues and was opposed to the entire concept of the baptism with the Spirit. One afternoon they were being pestered by several Arab men, following them. They went down an alley to avoid them and were distressed to see that the men followed them into the alley. Sensing that the men were up to no good, Kathy turned around and addressed them loudly in her prayer language.

She said the leader stopped dead in his tracks and turned pale. Recovering from his apparent shock, he then protested, "Lady, we don't hate the Jews. We don't hate the Jews!" and hastily departed.

This was a powerful confirmation to the doubting friend who later received the Baptism. However, back to the present, let's have Kathy relate her experience with an angel. . .

> **Angels often appear with manifestations of glory, reminding us of the awesome holiness and magnificent glory in which the Father dwells.**

MICHAEL APPEARS IN JERUSALEM
By Kathy Leshe

As I was preparing to go to Israel in the fall of 1999 to celebrate the Feast of Sukkot, I asked the Lord how I should begin praying in preparation. A prayer came into my mind that many years ago was prayed in the Catholic Church at the end of each mass. That prayer was, "Michael the Archangel defend us in battle. Be our protection against the wickedness and snares of the enemy."

Of course, when praying this prayer I did not understand that Michael was the chief angel over Israel, but I have since come to understand that truth from the book of Daniel. I began praying every day that the Lord would indeed send Michael.

The Feast that year was celebrated in the Hinnom Valley in Jerusalem. There were approximately sixteen hundred of us from all around the world gathered to worship. We came together on a hillside, while the worship team gathered at the foot of the valley. Behind them was a small building about a story and a half tall. As we entered into worship, many of us saw a huge angel in full battle array, at the top of that building with his sword drawn and stretched out over the valley. When we asked the Holy Spirit who it was, He replied, *"It is Michael."*

I cannot tell you how overwhelmed I was at the way the Lord had prepared this prayer for me, to pray in His will. God is so amazing. It was truly a time to worship.

Kathy Leshe
Worshiping at Sukkot in Jerusalem

Kathy Leshe: Wife, mother and grandmother, whose desire is to see the consolation of Israel and the New Jerusalem, resides in Florida with her husband and ministers with local churches to bring the fullness of God's promises to those in need.

LINDA CLARK

Linda is the daughter of Kathy Leshe and possesses a truly sweet spirit, which is quite sensitive to the Lord's leading.

Linda is a humble and willing worker, always ready to volunteer, lend a helping hand, or to minister to those who are hurting.

She is quiet and unassuming, and had I not asked, I would probably have never learned that she had encountered an angel. Many individuals, who have encountered angels, seem to keep the experience to themselves as something holy, personal, precious and private.

Fortunately, I did ask, and she graciously agreed to share her story . . .

Linda's account underscores the common angelic role of "ministering to the needs of the saints" offering guidance and protection.

AN ANGELIC GUIDE
By Linda Clark

In 1996 my Mom and I traveled to Israel to join with a group of Christians from around the world who were to gather on the Mount of Olives for three days of prayer, fasting, worshiping the Lord and of interceeding for Jerusalem.

During the event the organizers had planned a march around the ramparts of the old city to demonstrate our love for the Lord and our solidarity with the Jewish people. Dressed in white robes and carrying bannners, we proceeded to the Damascus Gate and the strairs that led to the ramparts. As many as three hundred Christians were participating in the march, but as we neared the Lion's Gate some of us became separated from the rest of the group. Now, finding the Lion's Gate locked and no available access to the ramparts, we stood wondering how we could manage to be reuinited with our group. Soon a young Arab boy approached us insisting that he knew of a shortcut to the top of the wall.

He brought us through the gate only to find that we would have to climb a wall in order to go any further. While many did attempt to scale the wall, my Mom and I prayerfully began to consider what our options were, what we should do, and what the Lord's purpose might be. Climbing the wall would be out of the question. Not only was it almost ten feet high, but with our white robes we were hardly dressed for wall-climbing. More important to us, however, was the issue of whether we were in the will of the Lord. We were now in the distinctly Arab section of the Old City, and as we continued to seek the Lord, my Mom came to believe that He was directing us to leave the group, continue walking down Derech Ha Ophel Street, deeper into the Arab section of the city and to claim it for the Lord.

As we walked down the street, Arab eyes followed us on every side. Whispering and jeers filled our ears and the heaviness of dark eyes were all around us. Although I was confident that we were walking where the Lord was leading, it occurred to me that our lives could be in jeopardy. Two women alone, unescorted, and wearing white robes. Well, I simply began praying that the Lord would protect us.

In what seemed like hours, we finally came to the next section of the wall, and as we passed through Herod's Gate, a man approached us. He asked why were there, unescorted, in that part of Jerusalem. We explained simply that we had been separated from our group but were sure that the Lord was leading us. He asked if he might walk with us until we came to the Damascus Gate. Gladly, we accepted his offer, knowing that it was virtually forbidden for Western women to walk alone in that area.

At last we were approaching the Damascus Gate. After we had exchanged pleasantries, we asked why he was in Israel and especially in this section of the Old City. He replied matter-of-factly. "I needed to be here."

Thinking to ourselves how odd this all was, our new friend instructed us to wait outside the Gate. He went on through and reappeared a few minutes later. The presence of the Lord surrounded us and we were overwhelmed by the man's concern and urgency for us. He told us it was time to go through the Gate. So we prayed the Lord's blessings on him and walked through the Damascus Gate. But when we paused to look back, he was gone.

We shortly found our group, knowing that God had sent His angel to protect and guide us.

Linda Clark
(wearing her white robe in the Holy Land)

Linda Clark is a homemaker and a home-school mom. She says her prayer is, "That our children would know and receive their full inheritance in Christ and that broken-hearted Christians would come to know that deliverance is for every true believer.

Prison Book Project
P. O. Box 1146
Sharpes, Fl. 32959

MICHELLE POTTEBAUM

Michelle came to my prayer room years ago, seeking more power for her life, which she received with the Baptism with the Spirit. She also wanted deliverance from some strongholds which had come to light as a result of her break up with Joe, the man she had intended to marry. After she was set free, we prayed for God's guidance for her future, and, if it was His will, to bring Joe back into her life.

Over the years she has brought or sent numerous individuals to our prayer room with a variety of needs. It has been exciting to observe her progress in the Lord and the blessings which God has showered both upon her and Joe.

Michelle had an unusual angelic encounter, which I asked her to share because her experience is very illustrative.

> **The Scripture admonishes us to not forget to entertain strangers: for thereby some have entertained angels unawares. In her case Michelle wasn't entirely sure that the stranger whom she met was an angel but did supect that was the case.**

WAS "JODY" AN ANGEL?
By Michelle Pottebaum

After days of coordinating a Fortune 500 company's business meeting, I had a few hours to regroup before returning home. The week had been hurried, with few moments to think about matters other than video presentations and handouts. But I found myself on my knees by my bedside in the beautiful Four Season Ocean Grand in Palm Beach Florida praying to God for direction.

It was a critical time in my life. The questions that surfaced from my heart to my head as soon as I had a still moment centered on work and relationships. I was months away from completing a master's degree to pursue a second career in counseling. Although I attended a secular institution, I had also taken seminary classes, and my heart's desire was to practice counseling from a Christian worldview. I was, however, unsure of *where* God wanted me to work. A former professor offered me an opportunity to counsel in her Christian practice. I also considered working for another reputable therapist who was not a believer. I cried out to God on my knees in that hotel room, "Where do you want to use me God? It's getting close to graduation; I need you to specifically show me, Lord. I'll do whatever you want me to do!"

Also, I was in my 30's and had never been married. A few years prior I had been engaged and painfully called off the wedding. I was currently dating a wonderful man named

Joe. But because of my broken heart from the past, I was hesitant to commit to any relationship that was not clearly God-sanctioned. After dating for several years, Joe and I did not have any conclusions about the future of our relationship and needed God's sovereign answer. "God I want what you want for me and Joe," was my heart's cry.

After praying, I had an hour to take a run on the beach, shower, and make my plane back to St. Louis. I was beat, and selfishly hoped I would get a nice comfortable seat alone where I could rest after the harried weekend. As the captain made his initial announcements, I noticed the plane was quite full, yet I was surprisingly alone in my row. As I closed my eyes I saw an attractive woman board right before the plane's door closed. She walked to my row and scooted past me to her window seat. We said hello, but I resumed my resting position, signaling I was out of commission for the next four hours.

As I started to doze, the woman by the window asked me a question about the Four Seasons Hotel brochure I had on my lap. I told her I had completed a business conference at the hotel. As a local of Palm Beach, she said she often went to the Sunday piano concerts held in the hotel. Convicted of my selfishness, I introduced myself. She then told me her name was Jody Hengle. I began to ask her questions about her work and her life. An amazing thread of commonality between us began to emerge. I told her, although I had been in business for ten years, that I was completing my studies to become a therapist. When I asked her profession, she explained that she had a career in business but was now a therapist. How ironic, I thought. Jody added that she practiced specifically from a Judeo-Christian world-view. My eyes brightened and I quickly told her that I shared the same beliefs and vision.

Information was exchanged back and forth rapidly. I learned that Jody, after a long career in business, went back to school and entered a private counseling practice with a few other Christians (just like the opportunity offered to me). Jody knew of professional therapists in Nashville where I used to live, she enjoyed some of my favorite authors, she did some work with the church, and she was currently writing a book to be published by Focus on the Family. Most importantly, Jody was a woman who loved Jesus, and her devotion to Him worked itself out in every practical area of her life. Never before had I met a woman who shared so many of my past experiences and future desires for my life.

We went on to discuss that as a woman in her thirties, she was preparing for marriage for the first time. I wrote the date of her wedding in my day timer, December 17, 1994, and promised to pray for their marriage. She was marrying a college history professor, whom she deeply loved. He was older than Jody and had never been married. They were marrying on Key West Island and then heading for Ohio where he had taught for years at the State University. Jody was in the process of closing her practice in Florida to join her husband in Ohio. In Ohio, she said she would be focusing on their marriage, the move, and setting up their new home and was not planning to open a practice at this time. I told her about my long-term relationship with Joe, eight years my senior who also had never been married, and she said she, likewise, would pray for me.

Hours passed quickly without a pause in the conversation, and I was disappointed when the captain announced we were landing in St. Louis. All fatigue had left me. My heart raced with excitement. Jody's life confirmed to me things I wanted for my own life.

As we both left the plane, I remember turning back to look at her walking down the terminal and wondering, "Did that just happen?" Did we have that much in common? Was she real or was she an angel?" I was left thinking. Through the conversation God showed me there are a limited number of soldiers in His army in the counseling arena. With Jody getting married and closing her practice, there was one spot available in God's army of Christian therapists, and I wanted her spot.

I returned home to my job and over the next few months finished my degree and accepted the offer to counsel in the Christian practice. My future would be difficult. It was not conventional to begin in a private practice setting. Most therapists start in an agency for a few years and build up a clientele before going out on their own. I would need to continue freelancing in marketing and public relations to pay the bills. But I felt directed, peaceful and sure. Also, Joe and I continued to date and began praying about our future.

I was overcome with gratitude for the insights that Jody shared with me and how much God helped me through her to make some major life decisions. I prayed for Jody on her wedding day in Key West and thought about her several times after. I decided I must write and thank her. I typed Jody a long letter and put it in an envelope. I only needed to get her new address in Ohio.

With confidence I called information in her husband's

hometown in Ohio and asked for their phone number under her husband's name. The operator made the search and responded that no such number was listed. Without a hitch, I quickly redialed information and asked for the university in Ohio where her husband taught. I got the number and contacted the school operator and asked for Jody's husband by name. The operator told me that there was no such name listed in the university. I patiently explained that this man was a long-term professor in the history department, and I specifically asked again for the listing. She searched and told me that no such man had ever worked for the university.

I quietly returned the phone to the hook. My normal lawyer-like intentions would have pushed to continue a more thorough search. But it occurred to me then, as it had after the plane trip… "Was Jody an angel?"

I tucked away the letter to Jody in my files to keep as a reminder of God's creative faithfulness to specifically answer our cries to Him for help and answers. He cared enough for me to send me an angel, who was assigned to speak my language, win my trust, and deliver a compelling picture of what life could be like if I followed God with a passion. She mirrored and confirmed to me my heart's desires. I left that encounter with clarity in vision and action in my steps.

My life has mirrored Jody's life in many ways. Since meeting Jody nine years ago, I worked for years in a private practice as a Christian therapist, taught in and out of the church, and married Joe the year following the encounter. We are convinced more than ever of God's sovereign plan for us to be married and both share a deep love for Jesus and for our four, soon to be five, children.

I believe Jody Hengle was God's angel sent to me in answer to my cry for direction. If I should ever be at a conference and meet an attractive woman by the name of Jody Hengle, I would be no less grateful for the way God divinely used a stranger in my life. But I stand convinced I will not meet her again on earth, but later in heaven when I see Jesus face to face.

Michelle And Joe Pottebaum and family

After a 10-year career in marketing and public relations, Michelle started a second career as a Christian therapist in private practice. She has a wonderful husband (married 7 years) and four (soon to be five) children. They live today in the St. Louis area, where she teaches a Bible study for women. Michelle says, "I love to see women fall in love with Jesus. I love Jesus and want to know Him better."

RUTH ANDERSON

One night thirty years ago, speaking for a meeting at the Anderson's Farm, I learned a very valuable lesson which confirmed a truth that the Lord had already been impressing upon me – that I needed to *hide His word in my heart* by memory.

I found that night that I was unable, because of the heat, to get close enough to the bonfire to be able to read passages from my Bible to illustrate the truths I was attempting to share with the large group of youth gathered for their weekly meeting. I was forced to quote the passages from memory. I learned that I would not always be able, because of lighting or other reasons, to be able to refer to my copy of the written Word. Therefore, I determined to learn the Word.

Over the many years since that night I have been blessed by reports of the Anderson's ministry to others, as well as to me. As an example, on at least two occasions, approximately ten years apart without having seen either of them during that time, Ruth, who often operates under a prophetic anointing, called me with "a word for me from the Lord." In over thirty years of ministry, I have encountered numerous well-meaning people who had "words for me" that were definitely not from the Lord. Yet, each time Ruth has called me out of the blue, her messages have been so right on that it has touched my spirit and moved me to tears, because the "words" referred to issues of which she could not possibly have been aware.

Recently, I was doubly delighted to learn that she had experienced angelic encounters, because not only was she willing to share them, but also because she is a gifted artist and attempted to graphically record what she saw . . .

Sometimes apparently angels appear simply as an encouraging love-gift from the Lord.

A LOOK OF DISTINCTION
By Ruth Anderson

The ground showed signs of frost and the air was crisp. It was the first Friday in November, and I was in my car driving to the inner city school where I taught art and music. The traffic had subsided. I was praising the Lord while driving east on Watson Road in St. Louis County, Missouri.

As I approached the overpass at Watson Road and Lindbergh Boulevard, my eyes were drawn to an ageless, tall, thin man. His feet were firmly planted on a small patch of ground next to the highway exit. The man had the look of distinction. His hair was white and his skin was flawless. He was wearing a gray suit, white shirt, black shoes and had a boutonniere in the lapel of his suit jacket. He held a black attaché case in his left hand ,and his right hand was resting on the ledge of the overpass.

I drove slowly past the man ,and the Lord said, "That was an angel you just saw." After driving about 300 feet I quickly turned my car around and drove back to the overpass where he had been standing so majestically. He was gone!

My eyes filled with tears as I praised the Lord for the wonderful surprise He sent me on that sunny frosty November morning. Hallelujah! What a day!

Exodus 23:20 *"Behold I send an Angel before thee to keep thee in the way, and to bring thee in to the place which I have prepared."*
First Friday of November 1979

EMINENCE

By Ruth Anderson

My gas indicator showed empty. There was nothing else to do but to stop at the local gas station to put gasoline in my car. The gas meter was ticking away, when I heard the sound of two motorcycles entering the lot of the gas station. A man and a woman were on one bike where they remained. The man on the other motorcycle immediately dismounted, stood straight and tall at attention and saluted me.

The man appeared as though he knew me. He was arrayed in a black leather jacket, pants, boots, gloves, helmet and goggles. All were immaculate. He was very tall, thin, had flawless skin and the look of distinction.

He removed his goggles and made a sweeping bow to the

ground before me. As he bowed, I had a quickening in my spirit from the Lord, who reminded me that this man and his two escorts were angels.

The man calmly got on his motorcycle, started the engine and drove off into a side road followed by the couple on the other cycle. I heard the roar of the motorcycles fading away to a hum as they went down the country road. My heart filled with joy to think that God sent three angels to bless me that day.

> *Bless the Lord, ye his angels, that excel in strength, that do His commandments, hearkening unto the voice of His word.* Psalm 103:20

May 2002

Ruth Anderson

Heritage Farm Fellowship is a non-denominational Spirit-filled home fellowship. The church began as a Bible Study in 1964. In 1968 **Youth For Christ** was held at Heritage Farm twice a month. **Heritage Farm Fellowship** became a licensed church in 1980.

Ruth and her husband Rev. Henry Anderson are both ordained ministers, who have served God by ministering the Word in hospitals, retirement centers, prisons and at **Heritage Farm Fellowship**. They have been married for 55 years and have three daughters and five grandchildren.

They hold a weekly church service and meet once a week for Bible Study. **Heritage Farm Fellowship** teaches and preaches the Word of God and the gospel of Jesus Christ. They give God all the glory!

Heritage Farm Fellowship
395 Heritage Farm Road
Pacific, Missouri 63069

THE MOST AMAZING, TRUE, MODERN ANGELIC ACCOUNT I'VE EVER ENCOUNTERED

THE ANGELIC BEGGAR
By Richard Burke

Richard Burke, president of one of the divisions of Citi Corp (parent company of Citibank), received the Baptism of the Holy Spirit in our prayer room and related to me a personal experience which he had with an "angelic encounter." His story was so dramatic, so inspiring and so enlightening that I asked him to share it at our little Thursday night meeting, and he has recently given me permission to put it in writing and share it publicly.

First he set the scene with a little background testimony:

"After being married for ten years, I went on a fishing vacation up to Maine with my brother, leaving my wife, my three-year old son and two-month old son with my parents back in New York. While on that trip one night I was notified by a State Trooper that my three-year old son had drowned in the trout stream that ran through our back yard. I immediately drove all night non-stop the 600 miles back home.

We were living in New York at that time, but we took my son to bury him in our family's plot in Washington, D.C. Over those three days I didn't eat or drink anything. I just shut down. The weight of my grief was unbearable.

I was raised as a Catholic but after leaving home had not

been in a church, with the exception of going only to please my parents when we happened to be visiting them. The priest who buried my son read the Twenty-third Psalm, and when he did, it really struck me. The Holy Spirit began working and revealing to me what a rotter I had been up to that point. As I walked away from the grave site, my sister put a Bible in my hand. My family and I had assumed that my sister was a "hippie." (Later I learned she was actually a born again Christian.) To the best of my knowledge that was the first time in my life I had ever held a Bible in my hand. I would never have let anyone else get close to me, least of all some Christian fanatic!

I had heard about Jesus at the funeral, and afterwards the Truth began to work upon me. I was unconverted at that time, but I became convicted. I soon began reading that Bible. I saw that the Apostle Paul was a murderer and realized I, too, had been a murderer in my heart from the time I was a child. I always wanted to be a fighter pilot (and you know what fighter pilots do). Fighter pilots do not merely joust or fly practice missions.

I was beginning to discover the good news. I had never heard the Gospel before, but someone finally told me the good news. We returned to New York after burying Jason, and I still had the rest of my vacation. I didn't know what to do with myself. I was 'unraveled.' I wasn't used to being unraveled; I was used to being 'buttoned up.' We got back on Monday, and by Wednesday I was thinking, "I've got to get my life together." I wanted to get back to my business career. I wasn't sure what to make of all of this stuff about Jesus. I didn't really know what to do with the Truth I had received.

Up to that point I hadn't had the courage to go into my son Jason's room. Wednesday evening I screwed up my courage and went into his room. As I sat down on his bed, something very unique happened. The Apostle Paul describes something similar in an off-hand way. Paul said, *"I knew a man in Christ above fourteen years ago, (whether in the body, I cannot tell; or whether out of the body, I cannot tell: God knoweth;) such an one caught up to the third heaven."* (2 Cor. 12:2) I feel my experience was not unlike his, but you can draw your own conclusions about what happened.

As I sat down on the bed, I was also "caught up." All of a sudden I found myself standing on the lawn, looking across the bridge from which Jason fell. Across the stream I saw Jason running from my right side toward the bridge. Jason was running and I was watching. I thought to myself, "Oh, this is an instant replay."

Standing on the bridge was a magnificent Man with a beard, in a white robe. He was a perfect man. As a Marine, I had measured men all my life, and basically there wasn't a man I didn't sneer at in my heart. I had never seen this man before, but when I laid eyes on Him, it was as if my soul rose up within me and said, "That's the leader I've always been looking for."

Jason ran up to Him. The Man leaned over as Jason reached up wrapping his arms around His neck and He picked him up. It seemed like it was another Jason who fell off the bridge. I didn't look at him. My eyes followed the boy going up into His arms. I realized that this Man was Jesus. He was there on the bridge. I was riveted, and at the same time experienced a sensation that was similar to taking a deep breath atop a high mountain in the fresh morning air. The air is so sharp, it just makes you feel good! I can still feel the sharpness of the air! That is exactly how I felt at that moment.

Then Jesus started rising up off the bridge with my boy! Up past the treetops. The next thing I knew, I was up and flying, too. I am a pilot and I knew that I was flying at about 10,000 feet, at a speed of approximately 400 knots, over a most beautiful land.

I have always loved the outdoors, hiking, climbing, trout fishing, bass fishing, and the like. This was a gorgeous land, with beautiful scenic mountains, and I cruised over it for about half an hour. Then I came down beside a lake. It was pristine. There were no roads; nothing but beautiful scenery. The lake looked like a pond with lily pads and dark water, reminding me of a lake I'd fished in Minnesota. Suddenly I saw Jason splashing and playing in the shallow part of the lake, having a grand time. Someone came into my peripheral vision, a bearded man, and stood next to him. I realized at that instant that it was my brother Roger, who had died a few years earlier. It was very peaceful. It was a beautiful scene, Jason and Roger were both at peace; they were fine. I realized I was the one with the problem!

After enjoying this scene for a few moments, I found myself in a dark place. A light was visible in the distance in front of me. As my eyes became accustomed, I realized that what I was seeing through the "dark place" was that same beautiful land, and that the darkness was some kind of a room which seemed like a tunnel. Then Jason walked out of the lake and came about halfway through the tunnel. But then he stopped, putting his hands up in front of him, as if feeling an invisible partition of some kind preventing him from coming further.

At that point I heard a deep resonating voice which I now take to have been that of the Holy Spirit, which said, "He cannot come to you, you must go to him."

About a year later I learned that those were the same words used by David after the death of *his* firstborn son. It was very precious to me, when some friends pointed that verse out to me. Shortly thereafter I found myself back on the bed and discovered that two hours had elapsed.

I was stunned in a very peaceful sort of way and had clear understanding: Jason is in a neat place. A place where I, too, would like to be.

I still had a grief problem and just that one cryptic instruction, I didn't know what to do with: "*He cannot come to you, you must go to him.*" This happened on Wednesday of the week that my vacation ended. The following Monday I returned to work.

I commuted 65 miles to work, an hour and forty-five minutes each day on the train. As you can imagine, that first Monday back at work was a hard day. All the people I worked with were flaming pagans and now something 'spiritual' had happened to me. I was isolated. My friends treated me like a pariah. Anyway, it was a tough day. In fact, every day after Jason's death was tough. I put in a long day, and then ran to catch the train for home. If I didn't make that train, it would be a two-hour wait. I just barely caught the last train out; the 6:05 out of Grand Central Station, and prepared for the 55-minute ride to

Groton-on-Hudson.

The train was crowded. Fortunately, I found an empty seat instead of having to stand for the entire trip as I'd anticipated. There was one bench seat open in the smoking car. I slid across it and took the window seat. Most of the other occupants of the car were occupied with *Wall Street Journals* and *New York Times*. About five or ten minutes into the trip, the worst looking beggar I've ever seen walked into the car and took the empty seat next to me. He was shabby looking; bad complexion, pale, bearded with gray stubble, appeared to be about 65 years old and literally dressed in filthy, shabby *rags!* What was even worse, he smelled really bad. The fans in the car weren't working, but fortunately the window was open. Knowing New York, I knew this guy was straight from the Bowery. He reeked...of urine, sweat, feces, vomit. It was terrible. I immediately said to myself, "I don't have to put up with this. I'm going to get up and go stand out between the cars and have a cigarette."

At that point, the Lord spoke to me in my mind and said, "You were a Marine; you can take it."

If the Lord wants me to stay, I reasoned, I'll stay, of course. But I thought that was a strange thing for Him to say. Then, I thought to myself, "I can put up with this smell; it's only for fifty minutes." I had been in some really awful places in the Marine Corps, and I knew this wasn't going to kill me. Besides I analyzed, "There is no way I can get up without it being obvious that I want to get away from him." For the first time in my life I had a thought for a down and out human being, "This guy is really down and out and has nothing going for him. I don't want to hurt him further." It was a radical thought: I was 34 years old and had never before had a compassionate thought like that in my life. I had never cared about anyone else, with the possible exception of my own family.

I'd never before seen a beggar on any of the commuter trains. So it was very strange to me that no one else seemed to even have noticed the presence of this foul smelling beggar who seemed so out of place.

When commuter trains pull out of Grand Central, they go underground for about 70 or 80 blocks before coming up above ground into the daylight. Shortly after the beggar was seated, the conductor came through the car to collect fares. All of us 'executive types' pulled out our wallets and flashed our monthly commuter passes. But when the conductor came to our seat, the beggar reached into his pocket and pulled out a roll of bills big enough to choke a horse. He peeled off a twenty and handed it to the conductor who didn't bat an eye, as he made change. You'd have thought that this conductor had beggars on his train every day. Something strange was going on, and I sensed it was somehow supernatural.

I didn't know what to make of a "wealthy" beggar, and my curiosity was definitely aroused. While we were still underground, I glanced over at him again. When I did, the hair stood up on the back of my neck, for *suddenly he was clean!* He was still dressed in the same shabby rags, but he was clean: he did not stink, was clean shaven, and looked to be in the prime of health. He now appeared to be about 28-30 and could have passed for a college football quarterback. This guy was just sitting there absolutely at peace. His eyes were clear, his complexion was clear.

He seemed totally unaware of my staring. He was looking straight ahead with one of those thousand yard gazes. I couldn't take my eyes off the man; he was so totally transformed. I spent the rest of the ride just staring at him.

Finally, I realized that he must be going to my stop at Groton-on-Hudson. When I say my "stop," that's literally what it was: the train stopped there. There are no facilities at the stop at all, nothing but a parking lot next to the Hudson River. The town is located two or three miles from the station (the stop) and so everyone leaves a car at the lot.

As we pulled into the station, everyone got up. The beggar stepped into the aisle ahead of me, and we were separated by a couple of passengers. The thought occurred to me, "This fellow obviously won't have any way to get to town, why don't you give him a ride?" Radical idea number two: "Why not actually do something for him."

When one disembarks at Groton-on-Hudson, there is a long glassed-in corridor and then a glassed-in flight of stairs leading to the parking lot. I was following him on the platform, and as he started up the stairs, I reached around the woman ahead of me to tap him on the shoulder to offer him a ride, and *suddenly he wasn't there anymore!*

He started up those stairs - but he never got to the top of the stairs. He was just no longer there. He couldn't have gotten away from me. I could see the entire crosswalks enclosed in glass. He had simply disappeared!

I really didn't know what to make of that. So I went out into the parking lot and got into my car. Remember, this is my first day back after Jason's death. I cried all the way back to the house.

As you might expect, ever since the previous Wednesday night, every spare moment I had was spent in Jason's bedroom. As soon as I got home, I walked to his room and sat down on the bed. I really wanted to be "caught up" again.

This was the second time I heard the voice of the Spirit speaking to me. He said, "Why are you weeping, Richard? Today you've been in the presence of the Son of God on earth... and you're weeping?"

It is difficult to put into words what that thought meant to me: to think that I had actually been in the very presence of the Son of God!

For ten years I thought that the beggar that came in and sat down next to me in that commuter car was Christ! As a result, I gained a great deal of comfort and strength from that thought.

The Lord then opened my eyes to beggars. He broke my heart for the poor. All of a sudden my natural eyes were opened. In New York I'd *never seen* a beggar. Can you believe that? I had worked for three or four years in New York and had never seen a beggar! Suddenly beggars were everywhere! And they really *are* everywhere, but the world has so steeled itself it doesn't see them. The beggars kept coming up to me as I walked down the street. It was great. I had such a supernatural love for beggars, I just kept giving them money. It became humorous. There was one particular beggar whom I passed regularly. Each time I'd see him, I'd give him a twenty. He finally got embarrassed and to avoid me, would cross the street when he saw me approaching.

* * *

It wasn't until ten years later that the Lord revealed the truth He wanted me to know and which I originally wasn't ready to handle. He revealed what really happened on that train and *who* the beggar really was.

The Lord very plainly said to me, "The beggar you saw on the train that evening *was not* an angel, and it *was not* the Son of God! That foul smelling beggar was... *you*: you, before I came into your life, and you after I saved and cleansed you!

"And he showed me Joshua the high priest standing before the angel of the LORD, and Satan standing at his right hand to resist him.

"And the LORD said unto Satan, The LORD rebuke thee, O Satan; even the LORD that hath chosen Jerusalem rebuke thee: is not this a brand plucked out of the fire?

"Now Joshua was clothed with filthy garments, and stood before the angel.

"And he answered and spake unto those that stood before him, saying, Take away the filthy garments from him. And unto him he said, Behold, I have caused thine iniquity to pass from thee, and I will clothe thee with change of raiment." Zec. 3:1-4

"But we are all as an unclean thing, and all our righteousnesses are as filthy rags..." Isa. 64:6a

CONCLUSION TO PART TWO:

Why is it that some see angels, and the rest of us do not? Perhaps some people are more spiritually sensitive, or attuned, than others of us; perhaps some have greater needs, and others may have risked more for the kingdom of God than we have.

I still have not yet personally seen an angel, but I have been blessed to come to know and to love all of these individuals who *have seen* them. They each received a visitation at a time when they were in great stress, need or while intensely seeking the Lord.

To see an angel, as I'm sure each of these individuals would hasten to agree, although a great personal blessing, is not a sign of sinlessness, nor of perfection. Consider some of those in Scripture who met angels, such as Balaam who certainly wasn't righteous. Even Balaam's donkey saw the angel, which is a humbling thought.

Angels also provide us a foretaste of heaven's glory and cause us to further desire to be preparing ourselves in this life to be as ready as we can for the next life. We should be seeking God for all that He has available for us now, to better prepare ourselves for Heaven . . .

PART THREE

A REVELATION CONCERNING HEAVEN

A Personal Vision of Heaven

MY TWO "BROTHERS"

The goodness of God!

Although I haven't personally seen angels, as I have mentioned, I have been blessed by God with having received supernatural revelations of His truth on numerous occasions.

It is important for us to recognize that there are ways that God has chosen to speak to His people, in addition to messages spoken by angels. Perhaps the method we are most familiar with is through His written word, the Scripture. Yet, He is also recorded as speaking by means of dreams, visions, and prohetic utterances.

I did experience a *vision* with surprising and enlightening implications.

It all began like this . . .

My Vision of Heaven:
A Revelation with Great Parenthetic Truth

MY TWO "BROTHERS"

In the summer of 1988 I was severely suffering from undiagnosed peritonitis and running a daily fever of 103 and higher. Just before being admitted to the hospital for additional tests, where my wife was to be told for the second time during our marriage that I would not live through the night,[1] we went on a vacation to Colorado. I was so weak that all I could do while we were there was to lae on the couch.

One morning as I was laying on the couch looking though a window up at clouds passing in the sky, I had a vision. I should perhaps mention that I am not prone to visions, being a very calm, logical and somewhat stoic individual (as those who know me can attest).

Like the Apostle Paul, I experienced a vision, but *whether in the body, or out of the body, I cannot tell.* At the time I wasn't sure whether I was dreaming, hallucinating from the high fever, or actually receiving divine communication, but later discovered it truly was a Divine experience.

In any event, as I lay in Colorado, suddenly, in my

1 The author's wife was first told that Bill would not live through the night in 1970, while he was a "teminal" cancer patient. The amazing account of God miraculously healing him and leading him into a healing ministry is told in the book *Alive Again!* Impact Christian Books, 1983.

mind's eye, I was back in Missouri, at one of the regular Thursday night meetings that I conducted. I was standing at the front of the meeting hall (in an old American Legion Hall Building which we rented), and suddenly I heard myself say, "Lord I want to come home to you." Without warning, I began to float upward; surprisingly, I didn't experience even a bump when I reached the ceiling, passing through it as though it were a cloud. I then began moving upwards at a very rapid pace and all the surroundings were pitch black. Nothing was visible; although I was conscious of moving upward with great velocity and had a conscious awareness that I was going to meet Jesus. But it was only a feeling. I had heard nothing, nor had I seen anything.

Abruptly my movement stopped and I was aware that I was lying prostrate, and I sensed that I was at the feet of Jesus. It was still pitch black, and I could not see Him, nor to my knowledge did I even attempt to raise my head. I think my eyes were shut; I was lying prostrate before Him in an attitude of worship, merely conscious that I was at His feet.

He spoke and said several things, and then asked, "Have you noticed your cheering section?"

Once again, without seeing Him, nor having any other clues, somehow, internally, my attention was directed to my left. When I turned my head and looked to the left, everything was still pitch black, but suddenly a brightly lit room appeared. It was as if there was an apartment building to my left with the front wall removed from one room, which was illuminated, and at first it was as if there was a theatrical scrim [a fine gauze-like substance used in the theater to create a dream illusion] in front of the room.

110

The lights came up behind it and the scene became quite clear: "My cheering section," as the Lord described it, was comprised of a group of people all standing in rows of about eight across, as if posing for an old fashioned family portrait. In the front row I recognized several of my deceased relatives.

The group began on the left front with my grandfather and grandmother joined by various aunts and uncles and friends. They were all standing very formally, posing in a rather dignified fashion, with not much cheering going on, I observed. And I later concluded that it was probably because I hadn't given them much to cheer about.

However, behind the back row was a dear and very fun-loving fellow Christian, who had come for several years to our meetings as a terminal cancer patient, and received a lot of deliverance and healing, with his life being extended for several years longer than expected. I had the honor of performing his funeral when the series of experimental treatments finally did him in. He was behind the formal grouping and was smiling broadly as he jumped up and down and wildly waved his arms. I sensed at the time that he wanted me to be sure to see that he had made it to heaven.

The Lord interrupted my thoughts by asking, "Do you recognize the two boys with your grandparents?"

My attention being directed back to them, I looked carefully at the two boys, each of whom was standing directly in front of one of my grandparents, who had their hands on the shoulders of the boy standing in front of them. The one in front of my grandfather looked to be about ten; the one in front of my grandmother looked to be about eight. However, I had no clue as to their identity and felt rather curious as to why they appeared in what the Lord Himself had identified as *my cheering section*.

I had to respond honestly, "No, Lord. I have no idea who they are."

The Lord stated simply, "Those are your brothers."

It made perfect sense to me at the time, although I am the oldest of my parents' three children. When I considered this dream, or vision, afterwards, attempting to assess it, I wondered, "Who could those boys have been? I have never had any older brothers, nor do I have any deceased brothers."

Then the thought struck me, "My mother once mentioned that she had a miscarriage before I was born." That could possibly explain one of these "brothers." In counseling bereaved parents and especially young women who had suffered miscarriages or stillbirths, I had assured them that they would again one day see those children in heaven, because we know that children in the womb have both a spiritual existence and a personality. [Consider John the Baptist, who at age six months *leaped for joy* in his mother's womb at the sound of the voice of the mother of His Lord, who was just three months old in the womb of Mary (Luke 1:41). And, that he was *filled with the Holy Ghost, even from his mother's womb.* (Luke 1:15)]

Perhaps, it was possible that one of those "brothers" could be accounted for by the miscarriage, but what of the other one? When I returned to St. Louis, I asked my mother if she might have had more than one miscarriage. She was surprised, but answered, "Yes, I lost another boy later on, about a year or so after your younger brother was born. He was so small we could barely tell he was a boy," she explained softly.

My mind reeled, God had indeed given me a vision, and had allowed it to be confirmed as true. But why? I believe the reason He allowed me to receive that revelation, about my two "brothers," was so that I might share it with you, that we might *comfort one another with these words.* (I Thess. 4:18) And that we might better appreciate the Lord's own love and compassion toward the little children, and the words He spoke in their behalf:

But Jesus...said, Suffer little children to come unto me, and forbid them not: for of such is the kingdom of God. Luke 18:16

Take heed that ye despise not one of these little ones; for I say unto you, That in heaven their angels do always behold the face of my Father which is in heaven. Mat 18:10

The good news is that one day we, who believe, shall be restored to all of our loved ones who have gone before us, and

*Then we which are alive and remain shall be caught up together with them in the clouds, to meet the Lord in the air: and **so shall we** [including you and even your children deceased before birth] **ever be with the Lord.*** I Thess 4:17

A Final Thought . . .

All that has been presented in this book merely confirms to us that which we should already have realized: that God is great, loving, compassionate, merciful and eager to communicate His power, encouragement, strength and truth to His people.

All of these accounts testify to the fantastic goodness of God!

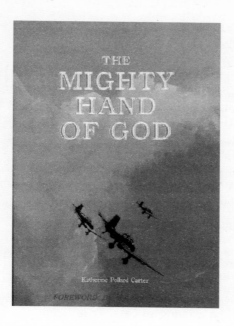

If you have been blessed by these accounts, you will also enjoy **THE MIGHTY HAND OF GOD**, which contains thirty-seven amazing instances where God has intervened in the affairs of men.

You will read some of the most outstanding and incredible miracles that have occurred in the history of mankind. Some of them have dramatically turned the tide of world events and affected the destinies of nations.

The outstretched arm and **THE MIGHTY HAND OF GOD** have miraculously protected and delivered nations, rulers, and world leaders and even humble soldiers who sought His aid. In response to faith, God's **MIGHTY HAND** has utilized visions, voices, angels and even the unseen forces of nature to answer prayer.

THE MIGHTY HAND OF GOD 216 Page Paperback $8.95
Plus 1.75 Shipping

EXCITING NEW BOOK
ANSWERS AGE-OLD QUESTION

The author draws upon the Scriptural patterns and keys
established by the Prophet Daniel to present readily under-
standable methods any believer can employ to *Tap into the
Wisdom of God*. He shows from Scripture that it is both
God's intention and will for man to turn to Him as the
Source of knowledge.

You will learn seven major keys to receiving knowledge
and find at least twenty-one practical encouragements to
build your faith to seek God for answers.

Plus a Revelation

Discover for yourself the fascinating and prophetic secrets
contained in Daniel Chapter Six, presented in the ninth
chapter of this book. Chapter nine, which is actually a
bonus book, presents an apparently undiscovered revelation
showing more than one hundred parallels between Daniel
and Jesus Christ.

"The most exciting thing I discovered was that what God
did for Daniel, He can do for any believer!"
P.M., Bible Teacher, Kansas.

$10.95 + $1.75 Shipping

Impact Christian Books, Inc.
332 Leffingwell Ave., Suite 101,
Kirkwood, MO 63122

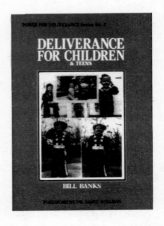

DELIVERANCE FOR CHILDREN & TEENS

   The first practical handbook for ministering deliverance to children.

   The material in this book is arranged to help parents in diagnosing their children's problems and in finding solutions for destructive behavior patterns.

   The **Doorways** section of this book illustrates how demons enter, and how they take advantage of innocent, vulnerable children. More than a dozen categories of routes of entry are identified, and examples given!

   The section on **Discipline** will be especially helpful to parents who wish to avoid problems, or remove them before they can become entrenched.

   The **Mechanics of Ministry** section will help you, step by step, in ministering to a child needing help.

   You will learn simple, surprising truths. For example...
* Easiest of all ministry is to small children! * Discipline is the most basic form of spiritual warfare and can bring deliverance!
* A child can acquire demonic problems through heredity or personal experience! * Deliverance need not be frightening if properly presented!

Do Your Relationships Produce
Bondage or Joy?

Are you in bondage to a person?
Does someone else manipulate you?
Are you easily controlled, dominated?
Are you tormented with thoughts of a former friend/lover?
Are you free to be all God intended you to be?
Have you bound yourself by your words (vows, promises?)
What are the symptoms of a Godly relationship?
What are the symptoms of an ungodly relationship?

Breaking Unhealthy Soul-Ties

deals with one of the most difficult blocks to spiritual freedom; the control of one individual exerted over another. While we may be blessed with God-ordained relationships, others can bring bondage to our souls. *Breaking Unhealthy Soul-Ties* assists the reader in diagnosing both healthy and unhealthy relationships, and offers positive steps to personal freedom. "Here at last is a thorough and theologically sound treatment of a little understood subject." From the Foreword by Frank Hammond, Minister/Author of Pigs in the Parlor.

$7.95 + $1.50 Shipping/Handling

Here, at last, is a thorough and theologically sound treatment of a little understood subject.
...from Foreword
by Frank Hammond

"I could feel the anointing, when I used the prayers contained in this book to help set a friend free!"

The authors of this ground-breaking book offer both
understanding and freedom!

mpact Christian Books

2 Leffingwell Avenue, Suite 101 • Kirkwood, MO 63122 • Phone: 314-822-3309 • Fax: 314-822-3325

Impact Christian Books

332 Leffingwell Ave., Suite 101
Kirkwood, MO 63122

AVAILABLE AT YOUR LOCAL BOOKSTORE, OR YOU MAY
ORDER DIRECTLY. Toll-Free, order-line only M/C, DISC,
or VISA 1-800-451-2708.

Visit our Website at *www. impactchristianbooks.com*

Write for *FREE* Catalog.